DISNEY'S

WONDERFUL WORLD OF KNOWLEDGE

Disney's

Wonderful
World of
Knowledge

THE DANBURY PRESS

THE DANBURY PRESS

a division of Grolier Enterprises, Inc.

ROBERT B. CLARKE   *Publisher*

THE STONEHOUSE PRESS   *Production Supervision*

ARNOLDO MONDADORI EDITORE

MARIO GENTILINI   *Editor-in-Chief*

ELISA PENNA   *Supervising Editor*

GIOVAN BATTISTA CARPI   *Illustrators*
CLAUDIO MAZZOLI

GUIDO MARTINA   *Author*

"Disney's WONDERFUL WORLD OF KNOWLEDGE"
is an updated and enlarged English version of
an encyclopedia heretofore printed in the Italian language by
ARNOLDO MONDADORI EDITORE, MILAN
and entitled (in English Translation) "Disney ENCYCLOPEDIA"

CONTENTS

ON THE SURFACE

Ah, here we are! That was a really smooth landing. Give me just a minute to close this umbrella. Well, here I am, Jiminy Cricket, ready and at your service. I must tell you that I've been chosen to be your guide in exploring one more world. You've already seen a lot of the mineral world and of the worlds of plants and animals. This new world we are about to look at is a very special part of the animal world. It is the world of man, the most advanced of all living things. Man, the inventor and builder of machines, is himself far more marvelous than any machine he ever devised.

I'm very proud and happy to serve as your guide to the study of man. It is a fascinating field to explore. It is the sum of all the worlds you have looked in on, and a lot more besides. Well, I'm all set to start now. Are you? Then let's go!

Opposite page: Part of a painting by Michelangelo on the ceiling of the Sistine Chapel in Rome. It shows the creation of Adam, the first man.

WHERE DOES MAN FIT IN?

Man (of course that includes women and boys and girls) is much smaller in size than many things in his surroundings, and much bigger than many others. Let's take a quick look at humans, to see where they fit in. You can start with the human being you see in the mirror. Beginning at the top, there is a roundish head, attached by a neck to the trunk or torso. Two arms and two legs extend from the torso, which is the largest part of the body. With some differences in skin color, shape of face, height, and so on, this is the human being that is found all over the earth.

As a rough comparison, man's size is to the size of the sun as an atom's size is to man's. Our bodies are made up of about 10,000,000,000,000,000,000,000,-000,000, atoms (1 followed by 28 zeros). Now imagine fitting people into the sun until it was filled to capacity. The number of people would also add up to about 1 followed by 28 zeros!

9

While we are dealing with numbers, here is another number that has to do with your body. No doubt you think of your body as a solid object. Yet 60 percent of your body is water! The earth we live on is also a lot more watery than you might expect. In fact, the oceans cover nearly three fourth's of the earth's surface.

MAN AND HIS OCEAN HOME

There is an interesting resemblance between the water in the oceans and the water in our bodies. Ocean water is not simply water. There are many substances dissolved in it. For example, there are chemical compounds called salts in the water. Ordinary table salt is one of these compounds. Dissolved salts of calcium and magnesium are also found. Bromine, iodine, uranium, and many other substances are there. There is even some gold!

Above: Old carvings and legends tell us that the study of the human body dates back thousands of years. This ancient Indian sculpture shows doctors examining and treating a sick patient.

Scientists who analyzed the composition of the water in the human body found that it resembled very closely the

composition of ocean water. This resemblance is not due to chance. All forms of life, including man's early ancestors, began in the sea. Our chemical makeup is a reminder of that fact.

Our bodies are made up of a large variety of chemical elements. Carbon, hydrogen, oxygen, and nitrogen are present in large amounts. But there are many more elements that the body needs in small amounts. Phosphorus, iron, chlorine, sulfur, copper, manganese, and a number of others are among those that the body must have to do its work.

THE SKIN, AN ALL-PURPOSE COVERING

Let's begin our look at the parts of the body by looking first at the skin. Yes, boys and girls, the skin is as much a part of the body as an eye or a hand. We all know what hands and eyes are for, but what does the skin do? It is easy to see that the skin is a cover for the inner parts of the body. But like many other organs of the body, it has several jobs or functions. The skin is an organ that senses changes around you, and helps to keep the body temperature steady. The skin is a barrier against germs. It also removes some substances from the body and stores others temporarily.

We really should talk about your skins, for you have two of them. The outer skin that you can see and touch is the

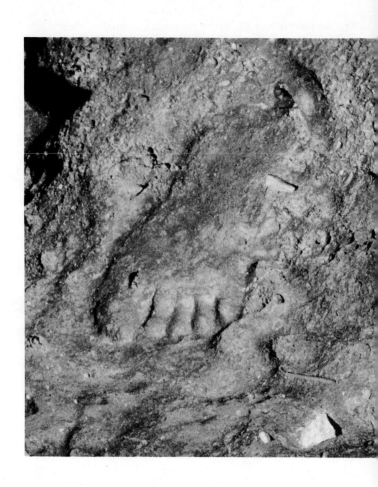

A look at the past. Above: A footprint of early man. Opposite page: Paw print of a bear made many thousands of years ago. Below: Artist's conception of some stages in man's development, from early fishes to Australopithecus, a creature both manlike and apelike, whose remains were found in Africa.

12

13

epidermis. It is skin in which the living material has been replaced by a hard substance called keratin. As you grasp, touch, rub, and wash, the cells of the epidermis are worn away. There is no need to worry, however, for the lower skin or *dermis* constantly produces new cells. These become fresh epidermis.

Tiny blood vessels in the dermis extend their branches everywhere. The body's nervous system causes these vessels to relax at some times and to tighten up at other times. The relaxed vessels allow heat from the blood to escape, and in this way the temperature of the body can be controlled. Body temperature is also regulated by the skin in another way—through the work of the sweat glands. Scientists estimate that the average number of sweat glands in the body is about 2,000,000. Each sweat gland is able to remove water and dissolved salts from the blood in the vessels. This is sweat, and it moves up in a tiny tube that opens through a *pore* onto the epidermis. When the sweat evaporates from the epidermis the skin and the body are cooled. Actually your skin acts like a built-in air conditioner.

Your skin is also an important sense

Opposite page: This detail from a wall painting in Pompeii shows a doctor treating a leg wound of Aeneas. In Greek mythology Aeneas was the great warrior who led the armies of Troy.

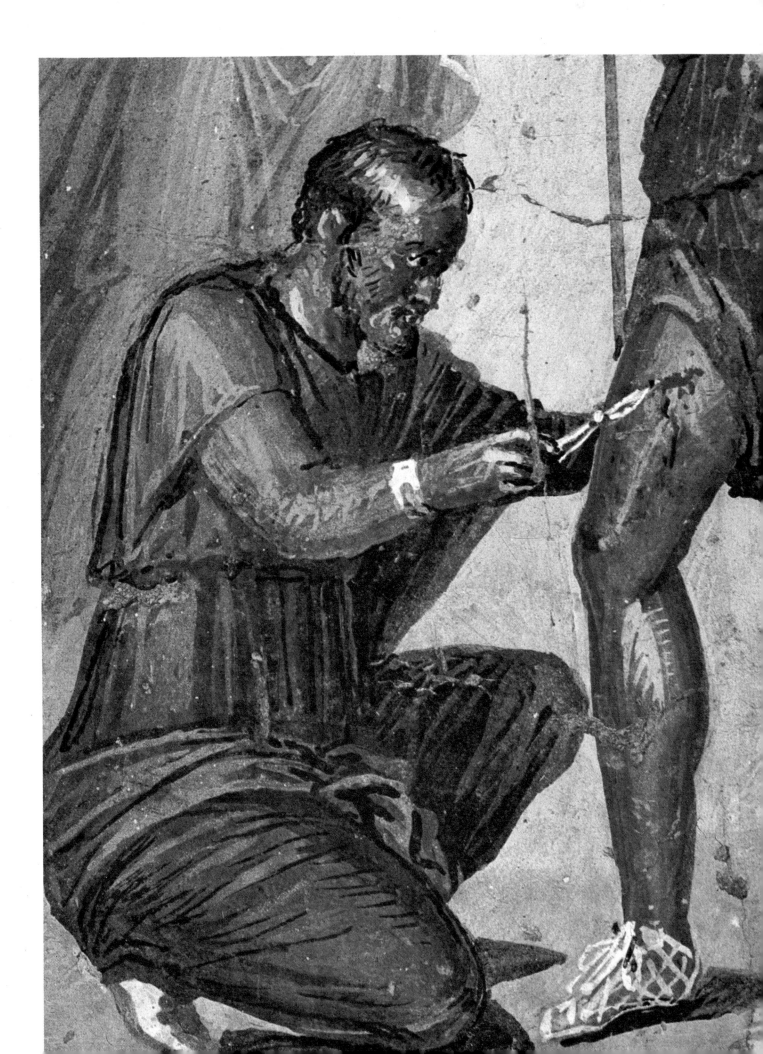

organ, like your eyes and ears, keeping you in touch with your surroundings. Is the water in the pool cold? Is the air in the room getting warmer? Nerve endings in the skin enable you to sense temperature changes. Other kinds of nerve endings in the skin are sensitive to touch, pressure, and pain.

The skin also has the job of growing your hair and nails. Long, narrow pockets of epidermis, called *follicles*, extend down into the skin. The cells at the lower end of the follicle divide to form more cells. These new cells form the hair.

Yes, boys and girls, the skin covers the body, but that's only the beginning of its work. And, now, if you're all ready, there are wonderful things to be seen inside your body.

Right: The people of the world come in many colors and shades. This group of pictures gives you an idea of the great variety of skin colors. Coloring materials (pigments) cause the color, and the same pigments are present in all races. The three main pigments are hemoglobin, which gives blood its red color, melanin, which is black, and carotene, which is yellow. Melanin and carotene are made in the lowest layer of the epidermis. An individual's skin color varies according to the proportion he has of each type of pigment. Shades of skin color vary too. For example, among lighter-skinned people, blonds have less melanin than brunets. Shades also vary with exposure to the sun. The skin of a person exposed to the sun produces more melanin, giving a darker or tanned appearance.

Below: Cartilage tissue. Most of the skeletal bones are formed from cartilage. Mineral salts gradually replace the cartilage, forming hard bone tissue. Bottom: Microscopic view of smooth (involuntary) muscle. Each elongated unit is a single cell.

17

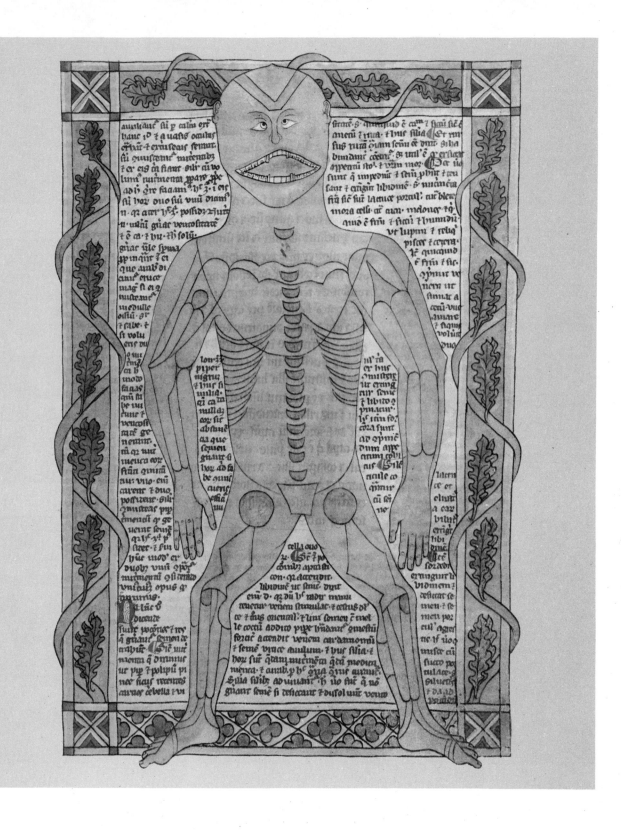

THE LIVING FRAMEWORK

Can you describe how your house looks? All right, please, let's not all shout at once. I can see you have a very good picture of your house in mind. You are probably thinking of how the outside of the house looks. But if you've watched a building going up, you know that the outside is the cover for a strong, stiff (rigid) framework of wood or steel. Your body, like your house, is built around an inner rigid framework, the skeleton. Your skeleton is composed of bone.

Most of your body is soft material, such as muscle, and soft organs, such as

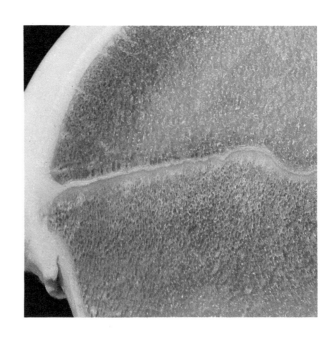

Above: Enlargement of section of bone tissue. Marrow of bones produces blood cells. Below: Framework of a fishing boat under construction resembles spine and ribs. Opposite page: Human skeleton, in an English manuscript of the 12th century.

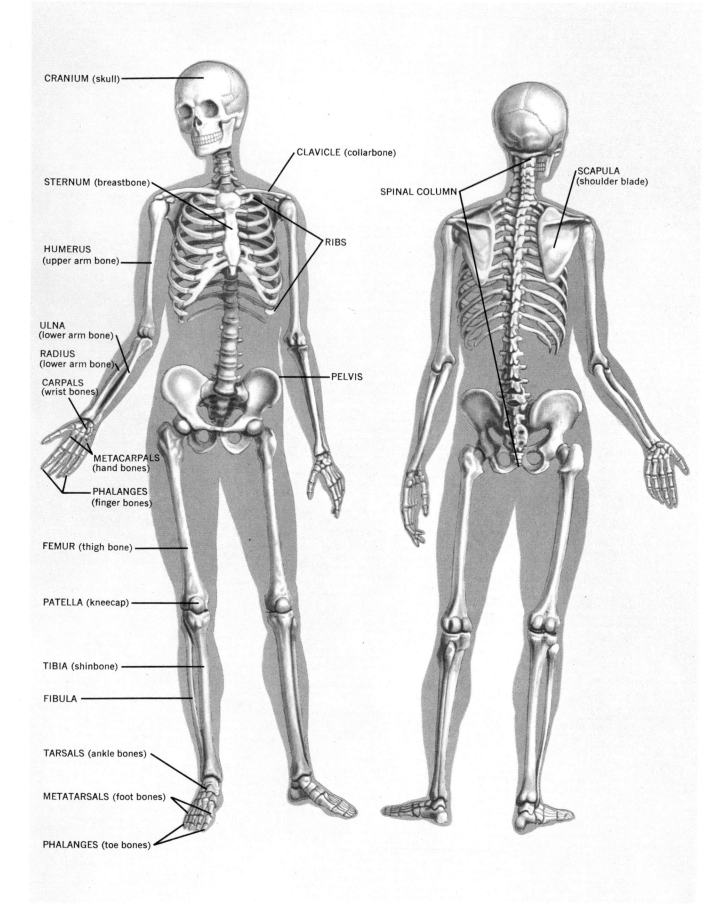

CRANIUM (skull)

CLAVICLE (collarbone)

STERNUM (breastbone)

RIBS

HUMERUS
(upper arm bone)

ULNA
(lower arm bone)

RADIUS
(lower arm bone)

CARPALS
(wrist bones)

METACARPALS
(hand bones)

PHALANGES
(finger bones)

FEMUR (thigh bone)

PATELLA (kneecap)

TIBIA (shinbone)

FIBULA

TARSALS (ankle bones)

METATARSALS (foot bones)

PHALANGES (toe bones)

PELVIS

SPINAL COLUMN

SCAPULA
(shoulder blade)

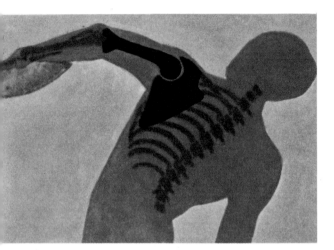

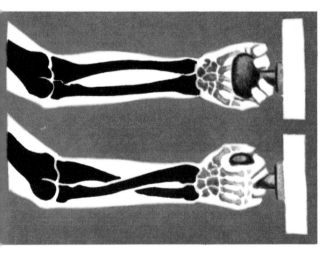

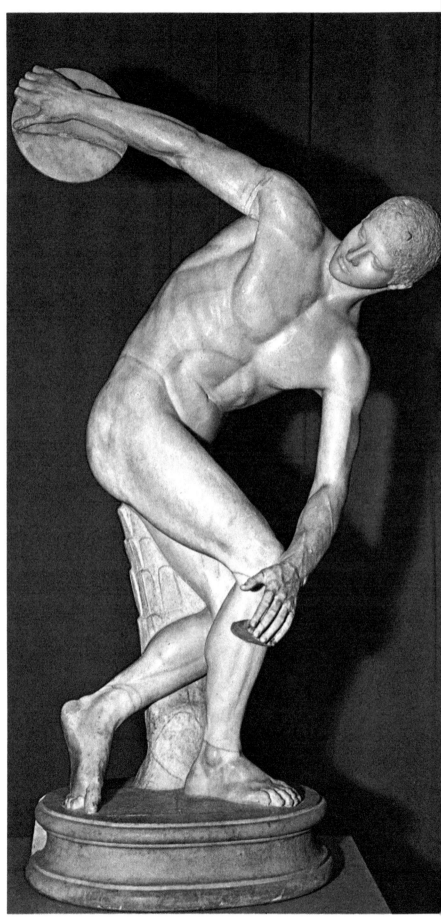

Opposite page: The human skeleton. Top: Ball-and-socket joint in shoulder allows motion in full circle. Above: Hinge joint in elbow allows bending of arm as well as turning motion.

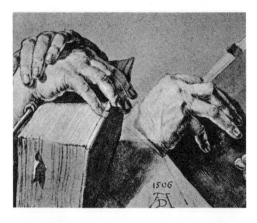

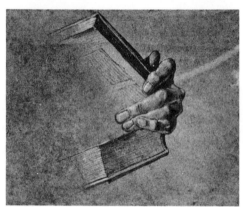

These illustrations of hands are all by the German artist Albrecht Dürer (1471–1528). He painted excellent portraits and watercolor landscapes. But he is best-known for his engravings and woodcuts and especially for his studies of the hands. The hands are most expressive, as well as being near-perfect anatomically.

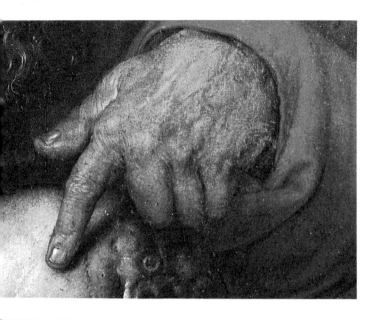

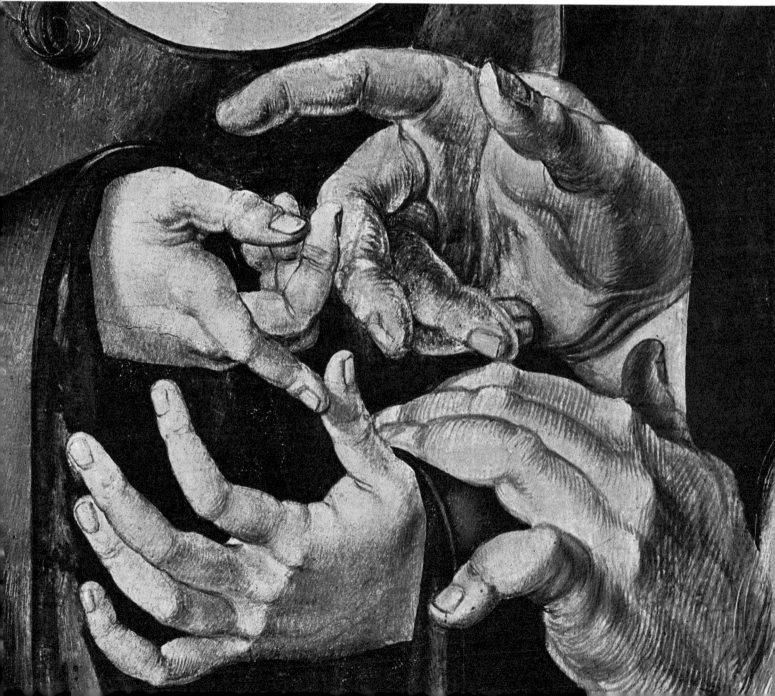

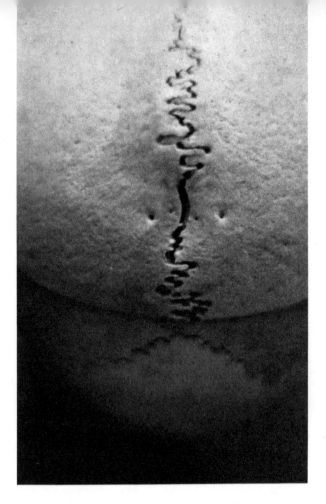
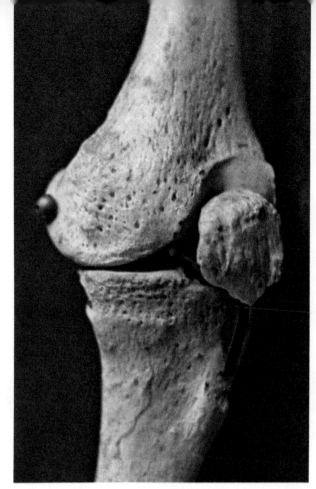

the brain or stomach. Without support from your 206 skeletal bones, you would be a shapeless mass, like a jellyfish. Some of the skeletal bones also have a second important job—they protect other organs of the body. The hard skull bones, for example, protect your all-important brain. Your heart and lungs, which are also vital organs, are protected by the breastbone and by the cage formed by the ribs.

The skeleton is a framework, but it's really very different from the framework of a building. Think of how much you've grown since you were born. And you aren't through growing yet! Can this rigid skeleton grow with you? Indeed it can! Bone is very much alive. Like the other parts of your body, bone has blood vessels and nerves, but it doesn't start out as bone. Did somebody ask how it does start out? Well, listen closely to a fascinating history.

When you were very, very young, in fact before you were born, you already had a good part of your skeleton. It was not made of bone, but of a softer material called *cartilage*. You still have cartilage giving shape to parts of you, such as the outer ear and the lower part of your nose.

Bit by bit the cells of cartilage were replaced by bone cells. Bone cells are just as soft as any other cells, but they can do a remarkable thing. These cells take dissolved minerals, mainly calcium and phosphorus, from the blood. They turn the minerals into the hard material we think of as bone. The cells surround themselves with bone, and continue to live inside their self-made bony prison. This process goes on now, too, as you go on growing. The calcium and other minerals needed to form strong bone come from the foods you eat such as milk.

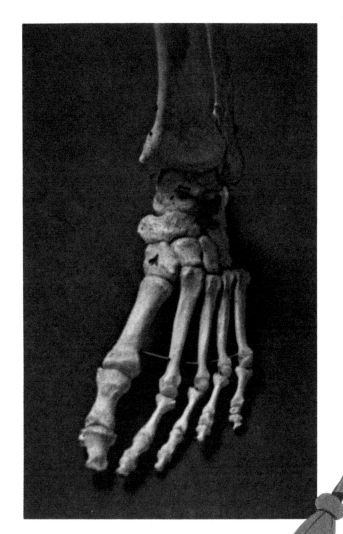

Opposite page, left: Joints of skull bones allow no motion, giving protection to brain. Right: Hinge joint of knee allows flexing motion. Above, left: Bones of the foot. Right: Part of the spinal column. Below: Ligaments (white lines in left drawing) tie bones together. Tendons (white lines in center drawing) connect bones with muscles. Muscles pull tendons, which in turn pull bones.

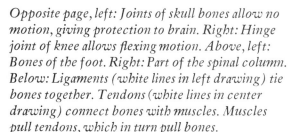

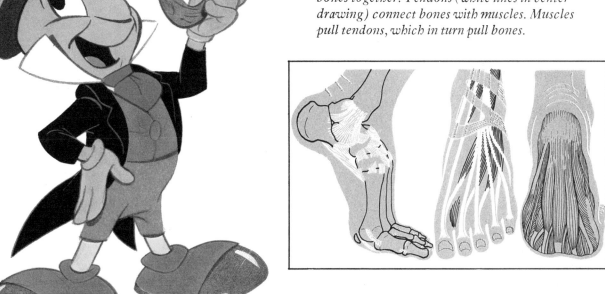

25

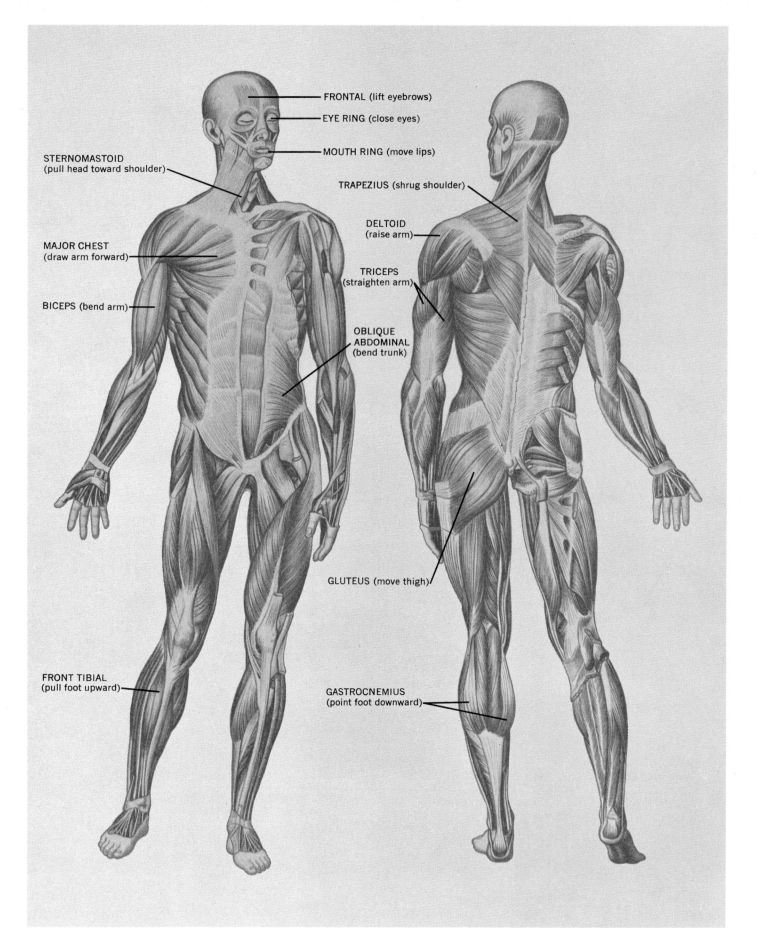

FRONTAL (lift eyebrows)

EYE RING (close eyes)

MOUTH RING (move lips)

STERNOMASTOID
(pull head toward shoulder)

TRAPEZIUS (shrug shoulder)

DELTOID
(raise arm)

MAJOR CHEST
(draw arm forward)

TRICEPS
(straighten arm)

BICEPS (bend arm)

OBLIQUE
ABDOMINAL
(bend trunk)

GLUTEUS (move thigh)

FRONT TIBIAL
(pull foot upward)

GASTROCNEMIUS
(point foot downward)

Have any of you noticed something strange about a bone that's been cut open by the butcher? What's that? You're right! The bone is soft and spongy in the center. You certainly are an observant bunch of people! I must confess I never noticed it myself. This spongy material is bone marrow. Marrow makes the bone lighter and easier to move, yet strong enough to support the weight of the body. Maybe you think support and protection are enough to expect from your bones, but some of them do something else as well.

The marrow is a kind of factory. Red and white cells of the blood are made there. What, did you think blood is just a simple red liquid? You'll see before long what a complicated thing blood is! In the meantime, let's look at the framework in action.

Your skeleton must be able to support you as you move yourself and various parts of your body. That's a lot harder to do than supporting something that doesn't move. The problem is solved by the joints that are located where bones come together. Different kinds of joints determine the kind of movements you can make.

The ball-and-socket is one kind of joint. Your arm and shoulder are joined in this way. The top of the arm bone is shaped like a ball. The ball fits into a shallow cuplike socket in the shoulder blade, much the way the ball in a ball-point pen is held in place. This arrangement, which is also found in the hip joint, lets you swing your arms and legs freely in a full circle. Another kind of joint is the hinge joint, which is like the hinges on a room door. These joints, such as the ones in your knee or elbow, allow motion mainly in one direction. The joints between the bones of your spine allow the

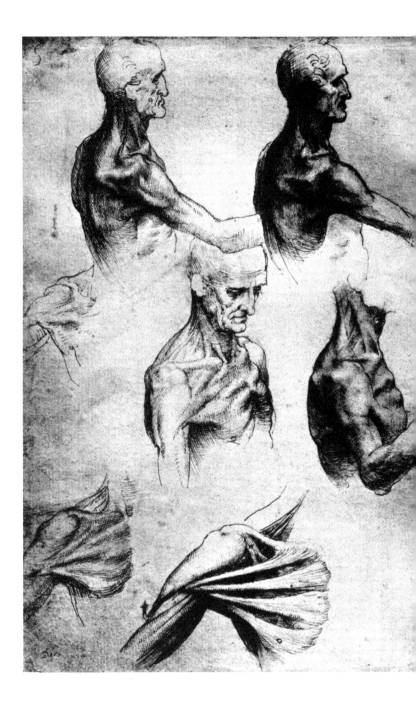

Opposite page: Muscles of body. Names and jobs of some muscles are shown. Above: Studies of the shoulder and its muscles by Leonardo da Vinci.

27

bones to move over one another with a gliding motion. There are even joints that prevent motion, as in the joints between the flat bones that form your skull.

Joints are surrounded by a case called a *capsule*. A special fluid in the capsule lets the bones move smoothly over one another, like oil on the moving parts of a machine.

THE MOVERS

I hope you understand that your bones take part in almost any motion you make. Action and moving bones go together. Yet a bone can no more move by itself than a stick lying on the ground can. Bones are moved by something, and this something is muscle.

A muscle is made up of cells that can pull themselves together into a smaller, thicker shape. When the cells do this, the muscle contracts.

What has all this to do with moving the bones? That's what I'm going to tell you right now. Bones are connected to muscles by tough, ropelike strands called *tendons*. When a muscle contracts it pulls on the tendon. The tendon, in turn, pulls the bone to which it is anchored, making the bone move.

Watch the front of your upper arm as you lift a few books or some other weight. That bunching up under the skin is your *biceps* muscle contracting. The biceps is attached to bones in the upper arm. When it contracts, the biceps pulls up the lower arm. Straightening the arm is the

job of another muscle, the *triceps*. It, too, is attached to the arm bones, but on the opposite side from the biceps. Most of your skeletal muscles work in such opposed pairs.

Dear friends, do you have any idea how complicated most muscular actions are? To throw a ball, for example, you must use many groups of muscles in your shoulders, arms, chest, abdomen, and legs. Each group must act in the right direction with the right force, in exactly the right fraction of a second! The director of these operations is your nervous system, which we'll talk about later on.

So far we have looked only at muscles that you control—voluntary muscles. If you take a little water into your mouth you can swish it around any way you like using voluntary muscles in your cheeks, lips, and tongue. But once you have swallowed the water, involuntary muscles in the food pipe and stomach take over. You no longer have control. Involuntary muscles throughout the body help to digest food, control blood circulation, and do many other jobs. One very special kind of involuntary muscle is found in the heart. Why don't we go there now?

THE HEART: A LIVING PUMP

Do you remember the last time you were in some busy place where the traffic never stops? Your body is a place like that. Even when you are fast asleep many things are happening. Muscles are working, nerve cells are busy, growth is going on everywhere. Billions of cells throughout the body must have supplies of food, oxygen, and other materials, and the wastes that the cells produce must be taken away. That enormous and unend-

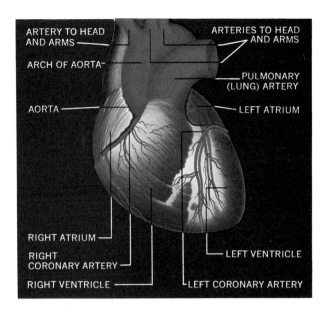

ARTERY TO HEAD AND ARMS

ARTERIES TO HEAD AND ARMS

ARCH OF AORTA

PULMONARY (LUNG) ARTERY

AORTA

LEFT ATRIUM

RIGHT ATRIUM

RIGHT CORONARY ARTERY

LEFT VENTRICLE

RIGHT VENTRICLE

LEFT CORONARY ARTERY

Above: Position of heart in body. Bottom of heart is tilted to left.

29

ing job is done by your circulatory system, which reaches every part of your body, from the tips of your little fingers to the tips of your toes.

The center of the circulatory system is the heart, an organ composed of powerful muscle. It lies within the chest, protected by the ribs and breastbone. About the size of your fist, the heart weighs less than 1 pound, but it does a staggering amount of work.

Each time the heart beats it pumps about 3 ounces of blood. That's true, Huey, 3 ounces doesn't seem like very much. But let's stop a moment and test your arithmetic. The heart beats about 70 times each minute. How much blood does it pump in 1 minute? Right you are Dewey, that's 210 ounces, which is over 1½ gallons. Now, which of you geniuses can work out how much blood is pumped in a 24-hour day? No adding machines, please. Ah, Louie has the answer. It is over 2,500 gallons, as much as a medium-sized tank truck holds.

No, Huey, of course you're not big enough to contain a tank truck full of blood. Where did you get such a silly idea? Oh, it's my fault. I should have

mentioned that pipes, or *blood vessels*, reach all parts of the body and return to the heart. So your 4 to 6 quarts of blood really travel in a circle. That's why the whole arrangement of heart, blood vessels, and blood is called the *circulatory system*.

Let's take a close look at the heart, the center of all the activity. There are four hollow spaces, called *chambers*, within it. A solid wall, or *septum*, divides the heart into right and left sides, so blood cannot cross from one side to the other. The upper chamber on each side is called an *atrium*. The lower chambers are called *ventricles*.

Blood returning from all parts of the body reaches the right atrium, fills it, and then moves down into the right ventricle. The muscular wall of the ventricle contracts, forcing the blood into the *pulmonary* (lung) *artery*. A *valve* that works like a one-way gate prevents blood from being squeezed back into the atrium. When the blood reaches the lungs it moves into the *capillaries*. Within these very thin vessels, the blood gives up carbon dioxide, the waste gas it picked up from the body cells. At the same time the

blood takes in oxygen from the air breathed into the lungs, to be carried to the body cells. Then the blood moves through the *pulmonary vein* to the left atrium of the heart. This short trip to the lungs and back to the heart is called the *pulmonary circulation*. Now the blood, carrying its load of oxygen, is ready to start on a much longer trip, called the *systemic circulation*, around the body. All aboard!

The blood moves down into the left ventricle. When the ventricle contracts, the blood is pumped into a thick artery, the *aorta*. Branches of the aorta lead to

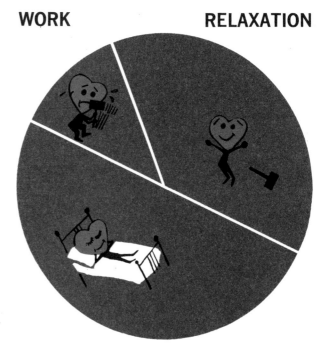

WORK **RELAXATION**

REST

Below: The heart is small but powerful. It pumps over 2,500 gallons of blood each day. In a lifetime of 70 years that adds up to enough blood to fill a huge skyscraper. The energy used by the heart during that time could lift a 10-ton weight to a height of 10 miles. Or, if you prefer to stay on the ground, the energy used by two hearts working for 2 years could send a small truck around the world. Above: Heart muscle works hard, but spends most of its time relaxing and resting.

various parts of the body. The blood, traveling through ever-narrower branch arteries, reaches capillaries that are woven in among the body cells. There is an exchange of gases between the cells and the blood. This time the blood takes on waste carbon dioxide, and gives off its oxygen to the cells. Now the blood flows into small veins that join to form the bigger ones that finally lead back to the heart, completing the circle.

The heart pumps the blood, on and on, in its nonstop circling. What was that, Dewey? Yes, the heart does get time to rest. I'm not surprised you wonder how that's possible. You must remember that the heart is working only when its muscles are contracting. But the atria and ventricles are relaxed most of the time, while they are filling with blood. So, in each beat, the heart spends more time resting than working.

The hardworking heart muscle needs a very large supply of food and oxygen. It gets what it needs from a special system of blood vessels. Two small vessels, called the *coronary arteries*, branch from the aorta. They lead back to the heart, where they branch to form smaller arteries. These lead to capillaries deep within the thick heart muscle, so every cell is well supplied.

The beating of the heart is controlled by a part of your brain called the *medulla*, and by special groups of cells, or *nodes*, in various parts of the heart. When you need more blood, as when you exercise, or less, as when you rest, the beat is speeded up or decreased automatically. Like a machine, the heart needs energy to run. Machines get energy from burning coal or oil. Energy for your heart and other muscles comes from burning fuel, too. The fuel is food. Ah, I see some of you looking happier. On to lunch!

MAN'S FOOD: THE FUEL THAT IS MORE THAN A FUEL

NUMBER OF HEARTBEATS PER MINUTE

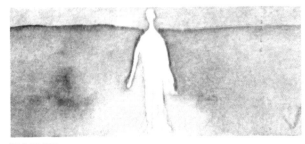

MAN 70

SWALLOW 600

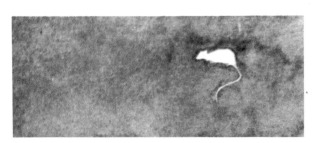

MOUSE 500

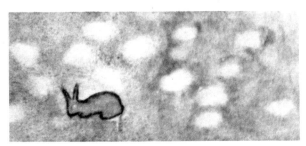

RABBIT 200

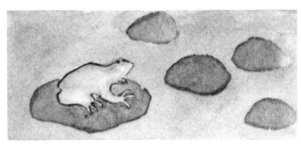

FROG 30

STEER 25

ELEPHANT 20

Among warm-blooded animals (all those shown above, except for the frog), the smallest animals usually have the fastest heartbeat rate. Small animals use oxygen more quickly for their size. Their faster heartbeat helps to supply the body tissues with more oxygen-carrying blood. Among humans, men have a slightly lower rate than women, and the hearts of older people beat more slowly than those of the young. Hard exercise may cause heartbeat rate to more than double temporarily.

33

Well, dear friends, wasn't that a fine lunch? I could see that all of you enjoyed it, especially Huey, with that third helping. This might be a good time to learn a little about the foods we eat, and why we have to eat.

When people talk about food and the body, they often compare the food with the fuel that is used to run machines. It's true! The food and the fuel are used in the same way. For example, gasoline is burned in the engine of an automobile

to provide the energy that moves the car. Some of your food provides energy, too. Your muscles use the energy to push, lift, and move things about. Unlike other fuels, food does more than provide energy. For one thing, we enjoy eating. More important, some parts of the food end up as new living material in your body, so you can grow. The food also provides material that you need to replace and repair worn-out cell materials. So you see, boys and girls, food is more than just a source of energy.

What's that, Louie? No, there is nothing magical about food, but it did seem that way at one time. Today scientists know a great deal about the food substances, or *nutrients*, and how the body uses them.

Before we learn about nutrients, let's look at a word everybody knows, but not everybody understands. The word is "calories." That's right, Dewey, calories do have something to do with losing weight. Can you explain why? No? Any volunteers to explain? Well, then, pay attention and you'll soon know.

Calories are like inches—they measure something. The inch measures length. The calorie measures the amount of energy in foods. You need a certain amount of energy to keep your body going, even if you are just resting quietly. If you move about a little, you need more energy for your muscles. If you run or do hard work, you need still more energy. You get the energy by taking in more food. Does everybody understand so far? Good. Now for the next step.

In your body cells food is combined with oxygen, and energy is released. Let's suppose you take in 2,000 calories each day. What happens if you use up only 1,500 calories per day? The unused food is stored as fat in the body, and your weight goes up. Now suppose you use up 1,500 calories each day, but take in only 1,000. Your body uses some of the stored fat, so you lose weight. Now do you see why people who want to gain or lose weight (sometimes it seems as if everybody in the world is doing one or the other) worry about calories? Such people should follow a diet that provides the right amounts and kinds of food for them. By the way, Huey, I hope you don't usually eat as much as you did today. If you did, we would need a weight-loss diet for you very soon.

Now let's turn our attention to the nutrients in food. First, there are the nutrients that give us most of our energy. They are the *carbohydrates* and *fats*. Carbohydrates include the sugars and starches. Candy, soft drinks, and the sweet desserts you love so much contain lots of sugar. Bread, breakfast cereals, potatoes, and rice are among the starchy foods.

Fats are found in large amounts in fried foods, whole milk, ice cream, butter and

Opposite page: Athletes at the start of the 100-meter dash. Hundreds of muscles throughout the body must be supplied with food and oxygen quickly to achieve this kind of action.

35

margarine, and in some meats. Ounce for ounce, fats give us more than twice the energy we get from carbohydrates. When a person wants to lose weight he usually cuts down on the carbohydrates and fatty foods. What's that, Louie? Yes, it's a shame but it's true, those are the foods that many people like the most. That's why losing weight isn't easy. So much for the energy foods. Now let's look at another group, the *proteins*.

Like the carbohydrates and fats, proteins contain the elements carbon, hydrogen, and oxygen. Also, like the carbohydrates and fats, they can be used for energy. But the proteins have something more which makes them very special. It is the element nitrogen, which is a part of all living material. Proteins must be available for the growth and repair of the body's cells.

I am going to tell you something about proteins that you will find hard to believe. There is almost no limit to the kinds of protein that exist. Many thousands of different ones are in your body cells. Many of them are different from the proteins of other people. Some proteins you have today are different from those you had a day or two ago. Proteins, in fact, make you what you are—yourself.

Tell me, now, did any of you suspect that your food could be such a complicated thing? And there's more to come. There is, for example, a group you hear a lot about—the *minerals*. Very tiny amounts of minerals are needed, but without them we cannot have strong, healthy bodies. One very important mineral is calcium. You need it for the formation of strong bones and teeth. Milk and cheese are rich in calcium. Another min-

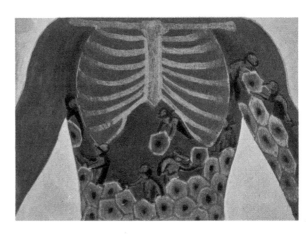

eral needed in bone-building is phosphorus, which is found in milk and eggs. Iron is needed to make hemoglobin, the substance that carries oxygen in the blood. Sodium, fluorine, and several other minerals are also essential. In addition, vitamins of various kinds are needed for good health. I can see that some of you are looking worried, and I know why. You wonder how you can get the right nutrients in right amounts without overeating. Well, stop worrying, and listen to your old friend, Jiminy Cricket. The answer to your problem is very simple.

Above: Small quantities of vitamins are essential to the health of the body. Fresh fruits and vegetables are excellent sources of vitamins. Opposite page: Vitamins are usually dissolved in the liquid part of foods. Chemists can treat the dissolved vitamins to obtain solid vitamin crystals, some of which are shown here. From left to right, and from top to bottom, they are: Vitamin C (ascorbic acid); folacin (folic acid); vitamin B$_6$ (pyridoxine); vitamin B$_{12}$ (cyanocobalamin); and vitamin B$_1$ (thiamine). All but vitamin C are part of vitamin B complex.

Painting of Bacchus, Greek god of wine. Bacchus was concerned with wine and pleasure, but the fruits shown with him would have been a good source of vitamins.

Food scientists have worked out a plan for each day's meals, using four basic food groups. Meals planned with the Basic Four as a guide will give you all the nutrients and minerals you need, and you won't have to worry. These are the Basic Four:

1. Dairy products: Two or more glasses of milk and some cheese.

2. Protein products: A serving of meat, fish, or poultry, plus a smaller serving of one of them, or an egg or cheese.

3. Cereal products: Three or four slices of bread, and a serving of breakfast cereal or of rice or spaghetti.

4. Vegetables and fruits: Citrus fruit or juice, and at least four servings each week of a dark-green or yellow vegetable.

The Basic Four will also give you the vitamins you need. And *vitamins* are exactly what we're going to talk about next.

THE ALL-IMPORTANT VITAMINS

Boys and girls, if we had the time I would love to tell you the fascinating story of the discovery of vitamins. It's like a mystery story, with a clue here, another there, and an ending where everythings fits together, and the answers are clear.

Ah, good for you, Louie. You want to know what vitamins are? They are chemical substances that the body must have. One remarkable thing about vitamins is that we need so little of them. Yet without these very tiny amounts we cannot grow properly, remain healthy, or even go on living.

Give me your full attention for a minute, and I'll explain why vitamins are important. All sorts of chemical reactions

Vitamin crystals under the microscope. From left to right, top to bottom: Vitamins A, E, D; two forms of vitamin K, vitamin C; vitamin B_1, B_2, pantothenic acid; biotin, niacin, folacin. The bottom six vitamins are part of the vitamin B group, or complex. Vitamin B was discovered in the early days of vitamin research. Later work revealed that the vitamin was really a group of vitamins. The names B_1, B_2, and so on were given to these vitamins. The group as a whole is called the vitamin B complex.

Percy Bysshe Shelley (left), Leo Tolstoy (above), and George Bernard Shaw (opposite page) were among the world's greatest writers. They also had in common a belief in vegetarianism. Vegetarians are people who rely on vegetables and will not eat the meat of any animal, fowl, or fish. Some vegetarians eat animal products such as milk or eggs, but others eat only vegetable matter.

SOME IMPORTANT VITAMINS

VITAMIN	SOURCES	USES IN THE BODY
A	Green and yellow vegetables, fortified margarine, whole milk, butter, eggs, liver.	Vision in dim light; growth; healthy skin and lining of the body organs.
Thiamine (B_1)	Meats, milk, eggs, enriched and whole-grain cereals.	Release of energy from food within the body cells; formation of substances needed in cells.
Riboflavin (B_2)	Milk, meats, poultry, fish, enriched and whole-grain cereals, vegetables.	Release of energy within the body cells; healthy skin.
Niacin	Meats, poultry, enriched and whole-grain cereals.	Release of energy within the body cells; healthy skin; vision.
C (ascorbic acid)	Citrus fruits, tomatoes, green leafy vegetables.	Strong walls in blood vessels; strong teeth and gums; proper formation of connective tissue.
D	Fortified milk, eggs, fish, fish oils. (Exposure to sunlight causes formation of vitamin D in body.)	Growth; formation of strong bones and teeth.

go on in your body cells. Most of them must go on very quickly. A chemist in the laboratory usually speeds up chemical reactions by using strong chemicals and lots of heat. But some reactions can be made to go fast by using substances called *catalysts*. Your body makes its own catalysts. They are called *enzymes*.

Now we're almost finished. You need raw materials to make the enzymes. The raw materials come mainly from the food you eat. And those raw materials are—ah, Huey knows! They are the vitamins!

Well, now that you know why vitamins are important, you'll be glad to know that you can get the vitamins you need by following the Basic Four guide to eating.

43

THE DIGESTIVE SYSTEM

Well, children, I hope that now you have a fair idea of the many things that your food does for you. But you must realize that food, in the form you know it, is of no use to your body. The food must be changed physically and chemically. The process that changes the food is called *digestion*. It begins at the moment you bite into a piece of food and begin to chew.

The biting is done by the *incisors*, the chisel-shaped teeth at the front of the mouth. Pointed canine teeth to the sides of the incisors help to tear the food. Behind the canines there are *premolars* to cut the food, followed by *molars* for grinding.

While you chew saliva enters your mouth from three pairs of *salivary glands*. The saliva moistens the food and adds a digesting chemical, containing an enzyme.

What happens in the mouth is very much like what happens in a chemical laboratory. A chemist who is bringing about a reaction usually uses chemicals that are in powder or grain form. The small particles dissolve more quickly than large ones, and dissolved chemicals react much more quickly than dry ones. In the "chemical laboratory" in your mouth, the teeth cut the food into small pieces that will dissolve quickly in saliva and other digestive liquids.

The tongue and muscles in the mouth

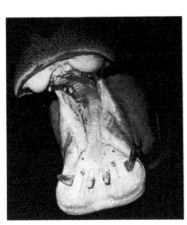
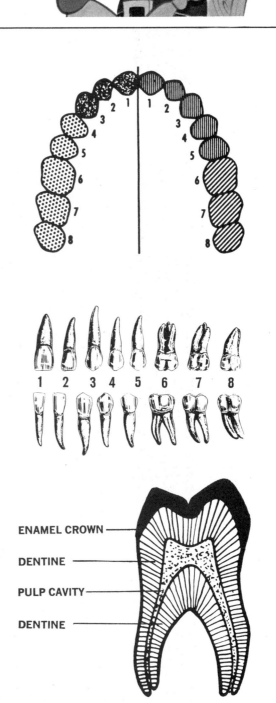

*Above: The teeth of different animals vary greatly.
Right: A human adult has 16 upper and 16 lower
teeth. The diagram is keyed to show you the name,
location, and appearance of the teeth. 1, 2: Incisors;
3: Canine, or eye tooth; 4, 5: Premolars, sometimes
called bicuspids; 6, 7, 8: Molars. The part of the tooth
that is visible in the mouth is the crown, and the
part that holds the tooth firmly fixed in the jaw is
the root. Upper molars usually have three roots,
lower molars have two, and all the other teeth have
one root. Children have a set of 20 "milk teeth,"
which are replaced by the permanent adult set.
Lowest drawing shows cross section of tooth.
Enamel is harder than bone.*

ENAMEL CROWN

DENTINE

PULP CAVITY

DENTINE

force the chewed food toward the back of the mouth. Once the ball of food is swallowed, involuntary muscles in the food tube take control. They push the food along until it reaches the stomach. The first step of the digestive process is finished. It takes less than half a minute. But for several hours to come, the food will be churned, pushed, liquefied, and treated with digestive enzymes. Finally the food will be in a form that the body cells can use. But wait a moment, now, I'm getting far ahead of myself. We're only just getting to the stomach.

THE LIVELY STOMACH

People have a hard time trying to describe the stomach. They often say it is J-shaped, and indeed it is. But the J is long and thin at some times, short and bunched-up at others. The shape depends on whether you are standing or lying down, on how much you have eaten, and on when you ate. This assortment of shapes is possible because the stomach is hollow. Its walls are layers of muscle. Food entering the stomach is squeezed, turned, and pushed about by wavelike contractions of these muscles. The movements, called *peristalsis*, also go on in other parts of the digestive system. That makes the digestive system a very busy place.

Boys and girls, I must explain why all this activity is needed. Several kinds of digestive juices are produced by the stomach and small intestine. These juices work on the food. The digestive enzymes in the juices must be thoroughly mixed with the food. Peristalsis does the mixing. By the way, the juices and enzymes are worth a close look. I promise to keep things very simple, because, like you, I'm not a chemist.

46

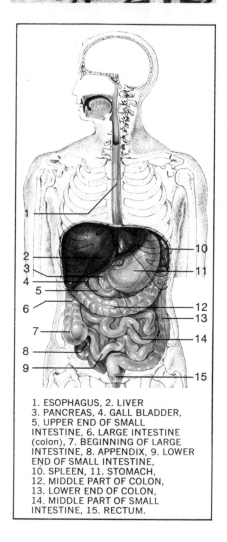

1. ESOPHAGUS, 2. LIVER
3. PANCREAS, 4. GALL BLADDER,
5. UPPER END OF SMALL
INTESTINE, 6. LARGE INTESTINE
(colon), 7. BEGINNING OF LARGE
INTESTINE, 8. APPENDIX, 9. LOWER
END OF SMALL INTESTINE,
10. SPLEEN, 11. STOMACH,
12. MIDDLE PART OF COLON,
13. LOWER END OF COLON,
14. MIDDLE PART OF SMALL
INTESTINE, 15. RECTUM.

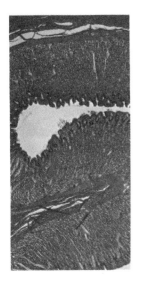 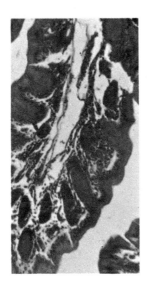

*Opposite: A portion of a papyrus document found
in Luxor, Egypt. It dates from the 16th century B.C.
and deals with medical matters.
Above, left: Microscopic view of stomach lining.
Right: Microscopic view of villus in small intestine.
Below: The digestive system.*

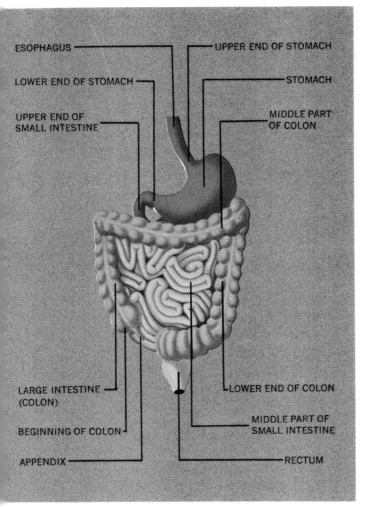

ESOPHAGUS

LOWER END OF STOMACH

UPPER END OF
SMALL INTESTINE

UPPER END OF STOMACH

STOMACH

MIDDLE PART
OF COLON

LARGE INTESTINE
(COLON)

BEGINNING OF COLON

APPENDIX

LOWER END OF COLON

MIDDLE PART OF
SMALL INTESTINE

RECTUM

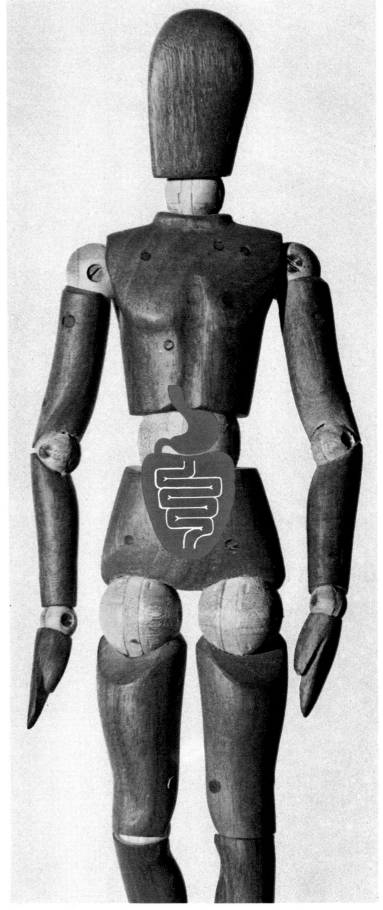

The juices are produced by millions of tiny glands that line the inner wall of the stomach. One of the juices is hydrochloric acid, an acid so strong that it kills the germs that get into the stomach in the food you eat. The acid also enables other enzymes to do their work. *Pepsin* is such an enzyme. It is a specialist, working only on proteins. I will just tell you briefly that proteins are very large molecules, composed of much smaller molecules called *amino acids*. The body cells use the amino acids to make new cell materials. Pepsin begins the chemical process that splits the proteins into these amino acids. The splitting process ends in the small intestine, and if you're all ready, that's where we're headed for right now.

THE NOT-SO-SMALL SMALL INTESTINE

Boys and girls, I once met a very tall man whose name was Mr. Short. You might say he was misnamed, like the small intestine. Your small intestine is certainly not small. It is about 20 feet long! It lies like a coiled-up pipe in your abdominal cavity. It is called small because it is only about an inch in diameter.

Like the stomach, the small intestine is a digestive organ. It is also an organ of absorption. Naturally you want to know what that means. Well, before we go into that, let's make sure we really understand what digestion is all about. You've heard me say that digestion makes food usable by the body. Just what does that mean?

When we talk about the body, we are really talking about the hundreds of billions of cells that make up your body. Each cell needs a constant supply of food from which it can extract energy and form new living material. Now, my friends, here is the first problem. To be of use the food must get into the cells. Only soluble food—that is, food that dissolves in water—can do that. There is also a second problem. The cell can use only small, rather simple molecules. Very little of our food has such molecules. Right you are, Dewey, digestion changes the molecules in food into small, simple, soluble molecules.

The main part of the digestive system is a long tube called the *alimentary canal*. It begins with the mouth and continues into the *esophagus*, or food tube, the stomach, and the small and large intestines. At several places enzyme-producing organs empty their juices into the canal. Digestion takes place as the food is moved along slowly by peristaltic action.

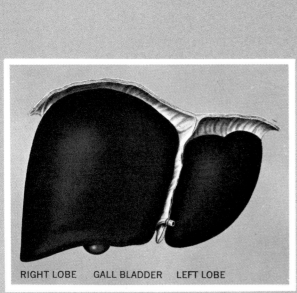

RIGHT LOBE   GALL BLADDER   LEFT LOBE

Above: The liver, largest organ in the body. Here you see the largest and smallest of its four sections, or lobes. The other two lobes are hidden behind these. Bile manufactured by liver is held in gall-bladder until it is needed in digestion. Right: Red area shows location of liver in body. Below: Cells of liver tissue, photographed through the microscope.

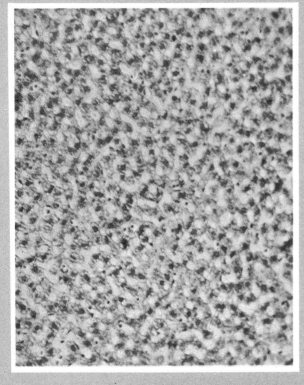

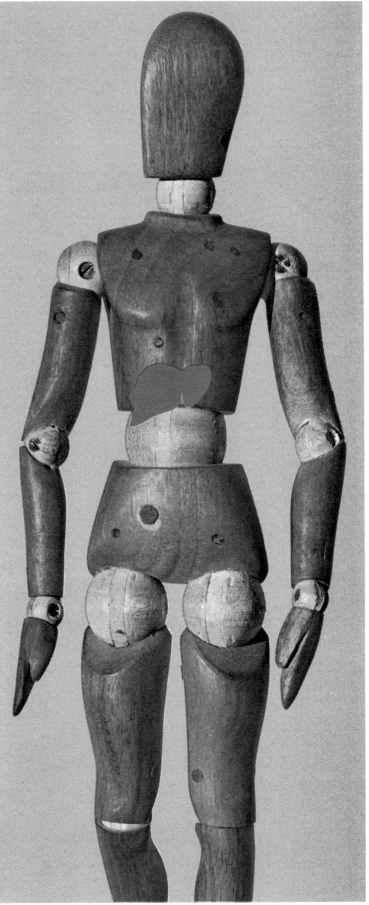

You remember that we saw the beginning of digestion in the mouth. Here the large, insoluble molecules of starch are attacked by *ptyalin*, an enzyme in the saliva. We also saw that pepsin, produced in the stomach, acts on the giant insoluble molecules of proteins.

The walls of the small intestine contain many tiny glands that produce digestive enzymes. There are also two large separate glands—the *liver* and the *pancreas*—whose juices enter the small intestine through a small tube, or *duct*. With so many juices pouring into the small intestine, it is no wonder that most digestion occurs there!

The liver and pancreas are worth an extra look, because they do a lot of extra work. The pancreas, besides producing pancreatic juice for digestion, is an endocrine gland. We'll learn later on what that is. And then the liver—well, children, the liver can only be described as a jack-of-all-trades. It does dozens of different jobs. Louie wants to hear about all of them. We don't have the time for that, but we really must look at a few of these jobs.

First let's find the liver. It lies within the right abdominal cavity, and it weighs between 2 and 3 pounds. The liver produces *bile*, a greenish-brown liquid. Bile is stored in a small sac, the *gall bladder*, until it is needed. Then the bile enters the small intestine through a duct. Bile breaks fats into tiny droplets that the fat-digesting enzymes can surround and attack. And, would you believe it, the liver also breaks down old worn-out red blood cells from which it gets the raw material for making bile! How's that for recycling materials? The liver stores *glycogen*, a starchlike substance, as well as iron, copper, and several kinds of vitamins. Like a chemical factory, the liver produces substances that are needed for

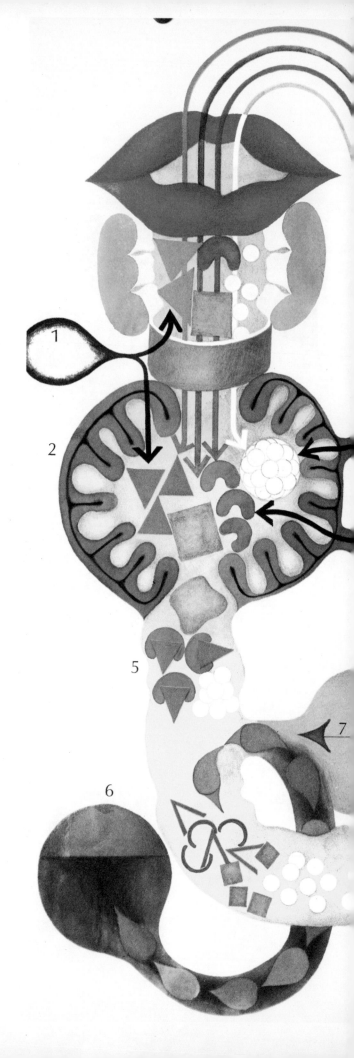

Digestion. Nutrients shown by geometric symbols. Glands in mouth (1), stomach (2), and small intestine (5), (8), produce digestive juices. The juices from gallbladder (6) and pancreas (7) enter small intestine. Digested carbohydrates and proteins, absorbed from small intestine, travel in veins (9) to liver (10) for storage, or on through veins (11), (12), to heart for circulation. Digested fats reach the bloodstream through separate route, the lymphatic system (13).

51

Above: Etruscan (ancient northern Italian) model of liver. Etruscans believed the liver could be used to foretell the future.

blood clotting, as well as another substance that prevents unnecessary blood clots. It also makes substances that keep you immune to certain diseases. The liver regulates the amount of blood that circulates through the body, and it changes certain poisonous materials to make them harmless. And that's only a few of the jobs of the liver. Quite a handy thing to have with you, isn't it? I know you'd like to hear more about some of the other jobs the amazing liver does, but we really must get back to the subject of digestion.

Nutrients are digested in stages in various parts of the digestive system. Some proteins, for example, are partially split by an enzyme in the stomach, while other enzymes in the small intestine finish the job. There are many in-between stages that you needn't bother your heads about. But you should know the *end products* of digestion, which is the name given to the substances the cells can use. Here they are:

- Starches end up as simple sugars.
- Proteins end up as amino acids.
- Fats end up as fatty acids and glycerin.

Several hours go by from the time you eat something to the time the food is fully digested. Peristalsis has moved the food 20 feet or more along the alimentary canal. Now, everybody please pay close attention. I am going to say something that will astound you. Ready? Would you believe that the food, after several hours, is not yet within your body? Dewey says it's impossible, and I'll admit it seems that way.

But let me explain. Imagine you are in a room that has a water pipe passing through it. There are no openings or faucets in the pipe. Is the pipe in the room? Everybody agrees it is. Is the water in the room? Not if you want a drink of water! In the same way, your alimentary canal, like a coiled pipe, is inside your body. The food inside the canal, however, is not available to your body cells. Then how can the food get to the cells? As always, your friend Jiminy Cricket stands ready to explain.

Do you remember I said that the small intestine is an organ of absorption? Now you'll see why I said that. The inside of the small intestine is covered with millions of tiny fingerlike projections called *villi* (singular, villus). The digested food, now in a nearly liquid form, moves past the villi.

Each villus is lined with a single layer of cells through which liquids can pass. Within the villus thin blood vessels absorb the liquids that contain the dissolved end products. The vessels lead out of the villus, and they join with other vessels. The end products are carried by the blood in this way, circulating throughout the body and bringing life-sustaining food to the hungry cells.

Some parts of the food, such as cellulose, cannot be digested. Cellulose is a tough, fiberlike material you have seen in such plants as celery. These materials move from the lower end of the small intestine into the large intestine. There water is absorbed from them, and they form solid wastes to be passed out of the body. But we are interested in following the digested food and in seeing how the blood transports it to the cells of the body.

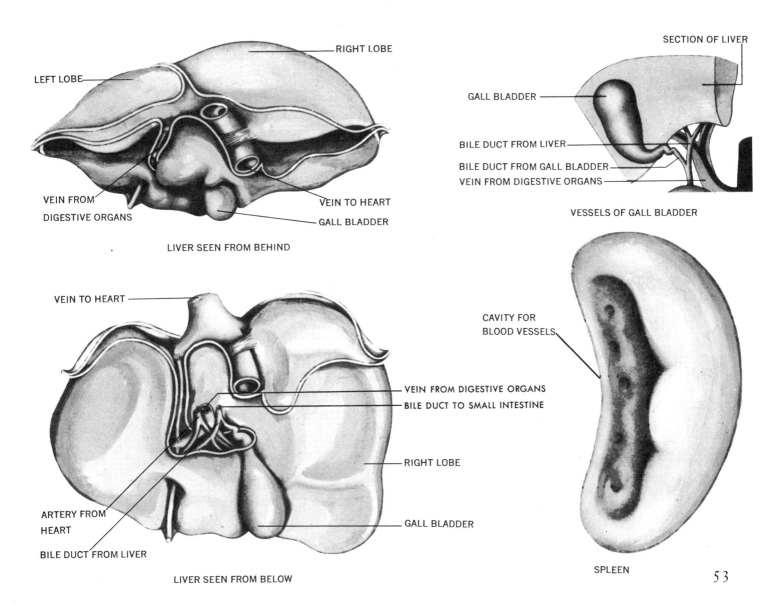

RIGHT LOBE
LEFT LOBE
VEIN FROM DIGESTIVE ORGANS
VEIN TO HEART
GALL BLADDER

LIVER SEEN FROM BEHIND

SECTION OF LIVER
GALL BLADDER
BILE DUCT FROM LIVER
BILE DUCT FROM GALL BLADDER
VEIN FROM DIGESTIVE ORGANS

VESSELS OF GALL BLADDER

VEIN TO HEART
VEIN FROM DIGESTIVE ORGANS
BILE DUCT TO SMALL INTESTINE
RIGHT LOBE
ARTERY FROM HEART
BILE DUCT FROM LIVER
GALL BLADDER

LIVER SEEN FROM BELOW

CAVITY FOR BLOOD VESSELS

SPLEEN

53

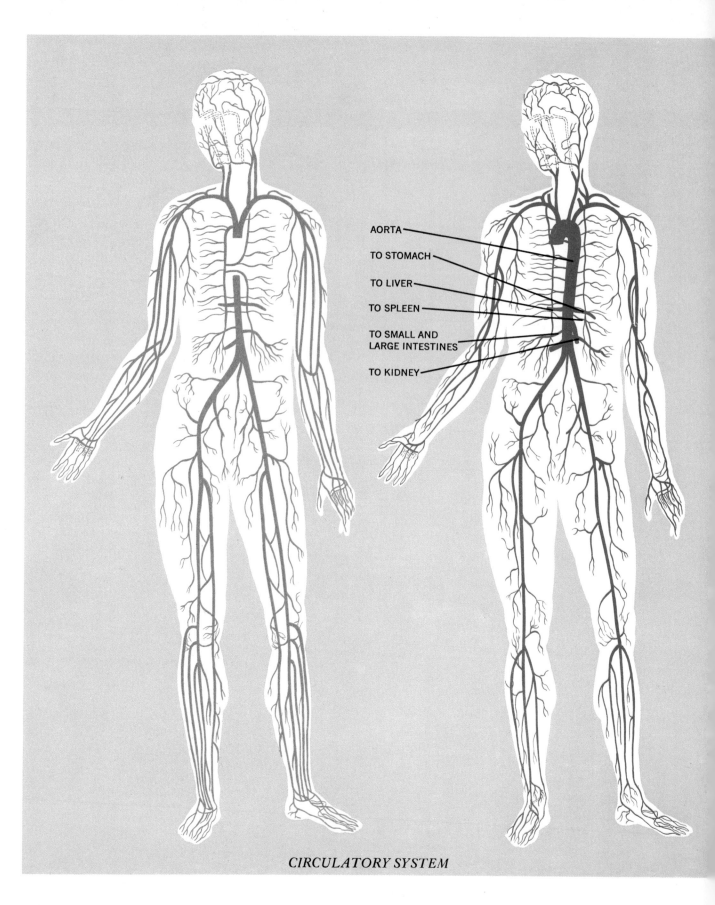

AORTA

TO STOMACH

TO LIVER

TO SPLEEN

TO SMALL AND
LARGE INTESTINES

TO KIDNEY

CIRCULATORY SYSTEM

Here you see how arteries (right) carry blood to all parts of the body. Blood returns to heart in veins (left).
A few arteries in abdominal area are labeled to show which organs they supply.

THE TRANSPORTER: THE CIRCULATORY SYSTEM

Boys and girls, we've talked about so many things. Let's stop for a moment and make sure we have them straight in our minds:

• Your body is made up of thousands of billions of microscopic cells.

• The cells combine food with oxygen to obtain the energy we need.

• The cells also use food as a source for making new living material.

• The only food that the cells can use is food whose molecules are soluble and small. That means the food must first be digested.

• The cells produce poisonous wastes that must be eliminated from the body.

• Food, oxygen, and many other materials are carried around the body by the blood.

• Blood vessels are the pipes through which the blood travels, pushed by the pumping of the heart.

• As the blood circulates it takes on and gives off various substances. For example, it takes on oxygen and gives off waste carbon dioxide gas in the lungs. The blood takes on digested food in the small intestine, to be carried to the body cells. Many other substances are carried by the blood. We'll look at some of these later on.

Doesn't the circulatory system remind you of a railroad? True, there are no freight cars, but the blood does a very good job of carrying everything that needs to be carried.

Can you remember the last time you cut yourself? Ah, Dewey remembers sticking his finger with a pin this morning. That will do. Dewey, can you describe the blood you saw? Let's all get this now. It was red, liquid, and thick. Those were good observations, but there are other things about blood that can be observed only with a microscope.

Actually only about half of the blood is liquid. The rest is solid—yes, solid. If you look at a drop of blood under the microscope, you can see thousands of round, pinkish-yellow cells. Massed together, they give a drop of blood a red color, which is why they have the name *red blood cells*. A drop of blood the size of a pinhead contains about 5,000,000 red cells.

The coloring matter, or *pigment*, of the cells is important for what it does. The pigment is *hemoglobin*, an iron-containing substance. This remarkable pigment combines quickly with oxygen, and it also separates quickly from oxygen. Can you see why this is important?

55

It means that the blood can pick up oxygen easily in the lungs, and drop it easily when the blood reaches the body cells. Blood cells wear out, so your body must produce new cells all the time. They are made in the bone marrow, while worn-out cells are destroyed in the liver.

I'll have more to say about the way in which your blood carries supplies to the body cells, but first, let me acquaint you with a defending army that circulates in your bloodstream. The "soldiers" in this army are *white blood cells*. The job of these cells is to kill germs. There is one white cell for about every 700 red cells. The white cells are actually colorless, so a special dye is used to make them visible.

White cells patrol the body, riding in the bloodstream. They can slip in and out of the smallest blood vessels. A white cell kills germs simply by surrounding and engulfing them. When germs get into the body, as in Dewey's wound, large numbers of white cells appear very quickly at the wound. In a serious infection of the body, the number of white cells in the blood may double or triple. This is one way a doctor can tell that a patient has some unknown infection.

Well, I can see that the battles between white cells and germs come as a surprise to some of you. Well, here's another surprise. There are tiny solid bodies, called *platelets*, in the blood. The platelets are part of a system that defends us against loss of blood. Dewey didn't lose very much blood today because the blood clotted. The platelets trigger a complicated series of chemical steps that end in the forming of a blood clot.

Heavens! It's so late I'll barely have time to tell you about the *plasma*, the liquid part of the blood. Plasma is thin and clear, and no wonder, for about 90 percent of it is ordinary water. But that other 10 percent! All sorts of substances are dissolved in plasma. There are dissolved wastes on their way to the lungs and kidneys, and digested food nutrients on their way to the body cells. There are enzymes and vitamins. There are substances called *hormones*, which we'll get to later on. And there are some remarkable proteins called *antibodies* that protect you from many diseases. Would you ever have imagined that one liquid could be useful for so many different purposes?

FRESH AIR FOR THE CELLS: THE RESPIRATORY SYSTEM

Boys and girls, I want to talk with you about energy. Agreed, Huey, that doesn't sound like the world's most fascinating topic. But it really is important to know at least a little about energy if you want to understand how the body works. I promise to keep it all very simple. Let me see now, where shall we start? I have it! Let's find out what energy is. Huey says it's power. Not quite right. Somebody else said strength. Not quite right, either. You know, sometimes things that seem simple aren't simple at all once you begin to think about them.

Scientists say that energy is the ability to do work. By work they mean moving or lifting something. It should be clear then that we need energy to move and lift things and to move ourselves around. Lots of other things that go on in your

Below: A quiet countryside, where the air is unpolluted.

body also need energy, although you may not see why right away. For example, your heartbeat requires energy, breathing requires energy, and so does keeping your body at the right temperature.

As I've said before, the body uses food and oxygen to obtain energy. Think of what happens when you light a fire. You use a fuel (wood, for example, or coal or oil). You use something else, too, although you don't have to supply it. It's already there. Good for you, Dewey! It's air, of course! More exactly, it's the oxygen in the air that's needed for the fire to burn. You know that as long as fuel and oxygen are available, the fire will go on burning, giving off heat. Heat is one of several forms in which energy exists.

Your body gets its energy from fuel (food, that is) in somewhat the same way. No, Louie, of course you don't see flames—there aren't any, luckily for you. But within every living cell fuel is broken down, and its energy is extracted. Like burning, this process must have oxygen to go on. A fire won't burn without oxygen, nor can the body live without it.

Boys and girls, can you all see how important it is that our cells get the oxygen they need? Life itself depends on it. As we saw, the circulatory system brings the oxygen to the cells. But the job of collecting the oxygen belongs to the *respiratory system.* Let's all take a deep breath and follow the path of the air.

The nose and mouth are the beginning of the respiratory system. Air that is taken in through the nose is warmed and filtered as it moves along. As you know, you can also breathe through your mouth, but then you don't get the benefit of the warmed and filtered air. The air continues down, passing through the *larynx,* or

58

We breathe in thousands of quarts of air every day. Exercise and play in fresh, unpolluted air are aids to growing up strong and healthy.

voice box, and on into the *trachea*, or windpipe. The windpipe forms two branches called *bronchi*. One bronchus enters each lung. Within the lung the bronchus branches, forming *bronchial tubes*. These branch in turn, until the smallest branches end in tiny hollow air sacs called *alveoli*. Each lung contains many billions of air sacs.

Imagine that each air sac is a tiny, thin-walled balloon. When you breathe in, air reaches the inside of all the balloons (air sacs). There the air comes very close to blood vessels on the other side of the thin walls. Oxygen passes easily from the air sac through the wall into the blood. At the same time carbon dioxide, the waste gas produced by the body cells, passes from the blood into the air sacs, to be breathed out.

Now, boys and girls, please brace yourselves for a couple of those true but hard-to-believe statements I like to give you.

In one day you breathe in and out about 12,000 quarts of air! This is possible because your air sacs have a total area of many hundreds of square feet!

Now, will everybody please breathe in? Hold it—not too long, I promise. Now breathe out. I compliment you on that fine performance. Do you know that it wasn't your lungs that did the breathing? Here is what happens when you breathe. Your ribs and breastbone are lifted by muscles, making the space within the chest slightly bigger. As this happens the *diaphragm*, an arched muscle like an open umbrella under the lungs, moves down. That makes the space within the chest bigger still. The air pressure within the chest is lowered, and the air pressure on the outside forces air into the lungs. When the diaphragm and other muscles make the space smaller, the air is pushed out of the lungs. Your nervous system controls these movements automatically. 59

AN ENDLESS CLEANUP: THE EXCRETORY ORGANS

Boys and girls, have any of you ever had to fire up a coal stove? Ah, just as I thought, you haven't. Let me tell you, you're very lucky. I mention the stove because it will make our discussion easier. No, it isn't true that you know nothing about coal stoves. You know that they use coal as fuel. And you know that the fire won't burn unless oxygen is available. And you know that the burning of the fuel produces wastes, even if you're not quite sure what they are. Well, there is waste carbon dioxide gas and water vapor, which go up the chimney. And there is a solid material, the ashes, left in the stove. People who use coal stoves must be sure the chimney is not blocked, so the gases can escape, and they must remove the ashes every so often. If the wastes are allowed to collect, the fire won't burn.

Louie wants to know why the wastes interfere with the fire. Fire is a chemical reaction. One chemical, the fuel, combines with another, which is the oxygen in the air. This chemical reaction, which happens very fast, is the burning. Some other chemicals, carbon dioxide for example, can stop the reaction, putting out the fire. You're right, Huey, that's why carbon dioxide is used in some kinds of fire extinguishers.

Yes, Dewey, at this very second I am coming to what all this has to do with you. Like the stove, your body produces a variety of wastes, and there must be some way to get rid of them. The job is done by the *excretory organs*. ("Excretory" comes from words that mean "to sift out" or "discharge.")

Opposite page: Ribs and diaphragm (solid black line) operate together in breathing. At left, they enlarge chest cavity, causing inhalation. At right, their action forces air from lungs. Above: Albrecht Dürer, in self-portrait, points to his sick spleen.

Now Dewey is asking why we have to get rid of our wastes, since there are no fires in us. Well, I don't want to get into complicated chemical discussions, and anyhow I don't know very much about chemistry. But you can understand what the problem is. Every living cell carries on chemical reactions, like a tiny chemical plant. These reactions keep the cell alive and in good health, but they can be stopped by certain chemicals, just as the fire can be stopped. If this happens the cell dies. The chemical that causes this to happen is said to be a poison.

As your body cells carry on their chemical reactions they produce certain chemicals for themselves or for other cells. But they also produce some chemicals that could act as poisons if they collected in large enough amounts. These are the

62

wastes that must be removed if the cells are to remain alive and healthy. Well, that was a long speech, Dewey. I hope it answered your question.

Boys and girls, you are asking some very good questions today. Don't be shy about asking more. Well now, back to the excretory organs. While a fire produces several kinds of wastes, you produce many more kinds of waste. Let's list a few of them:

- Solid wastes
- Carbon dioxide gas
- Water
- Salts of sodium, potassium, chlorine, and phosphorus
- Ammonia
- Urea

Huey, you're quite right to complain. I've been talking all this time about the excretory organs, without even a hint of which ones they are. Well, there are . . . let me see . . . four of them. And say, do you know, you're already acquainted with three of the four?

First, there are the lungs. You probably think of them as the organs that take in oxygen. They do that, of course, but they also excrete carbon dioxide, a job which is no less important. The lungs also give off water vapor (that's the cloud you see when you breathe out on a cold day) and some heat. Just hold your hand close to your mouth, breathe, and you'll feel the heat. Right? Now for the next excretory organ.

Do you remember our talk about the sweat glands in the skin? I told you that these glands help to regulate the body temperature. On a hot day the sweat glands produce sweat, which is mainly water with various salts dissolved in it. The sweat evaporates, cooling the skin as it does so. Heat and a little carbon dioxide are also given off by the skin. So you see

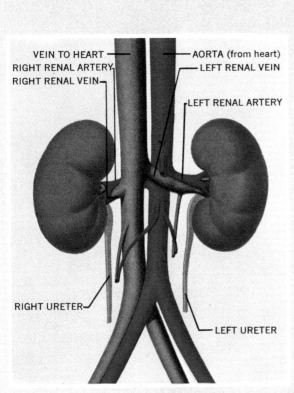

VEIN TO HEART — — AORTA (from heart)
RIGHT RENAL ARTERY — LEFT RENAL VEIN
RIGHT RENAL VEIN — LEFT RENAL ARTERY

RIGHT URETER

LEFT URETER

Above: The kidneys. Blood reaches kidneys through renal arteries. Kidneys remove dissolved wastes from blood, which returns to circulatory system through renal veins. Urine passes through ureters for storage in bladder. Below: Microscopic view of skin shows sweat gland tubules (left) and hair follicles (doughnut-shaped ring) at right. Right: red areas show location of kidneys.

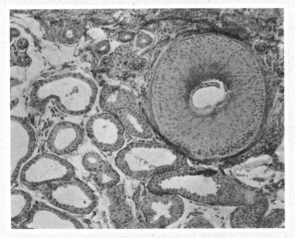

that the skin really qualifiies as an organ of excretion.

The third organ of excretion is the alimentary canal, or rather its last part, the large intestine. As I mentioned before, some parts of our food are not digestible. Cellulose in fruits and vegetables, and certain animal fibers, are examples. Of course these materials move along the alimentary canal with the rest of the food, in a semiliquid condition. But the indigestible parts are not absorbed like the rest of the food. Finally, at the end of the small intestine, the undigested material enters the large intestine, which is about 5 feet long and a bit over 2 inches wide. A great deal of water is absorbed from the intestine into the bloodstream. That leaves the undigested food as a more or less solid material to be passed out of the body. Some water, salts, and heat are lost at the same time.

Well, boys and girls, only one more organ of excretion remains to be looked at. I assure you, this one will amaze you with the way it is made and with the way it works. Actually it (or rather they, for it is a pair) forms the most important organ of excretion, the kidneys. One kidney is located on each side of the spine, in the small of your back. A kidney is a red, bean-shaped organ about 4 inches long.

Let's go back a moment to our study of the lungs. Do you remember the tiny balloonlike air sacs? Their very thin walls allow oxygen and carbon dioxide to pass through easily. Well, something of the same sort exists in the kidneys.

Each kidney contains more than 1,000,000 little filters called *nephrons*. A nephron is shaped somewhat like a cup of very thin china. The cup holds a network of tiny blood vessels. As the blood moves through the vessels, water, along with various dissolved wastes, passes through the thin walls into long narrow tubes.

In a 24-hour day nearly 200 quarts of water are taken from the blood in this way. All but about 1 percent of the water returns to the blood. The wastes, dissolved in the remaining 1 percent, form *urine*, which passes down the tubes to larger collecting tubes. Ammonia, urea, and other cell poisons are among the wastes. These substances result mainly from the breakdown of protein material in the body.

The urine collects in a central part of the kidney, and passes into a tube called a *ureter*. One ureter from each kidney leads to a muscular baglike reservoir, the *urinary bladder*. The urine is stored there until it passes out of the body through another tube, the *urethra*. And that, boys and girls, ends our look into the way harmful substances are removed from the body.

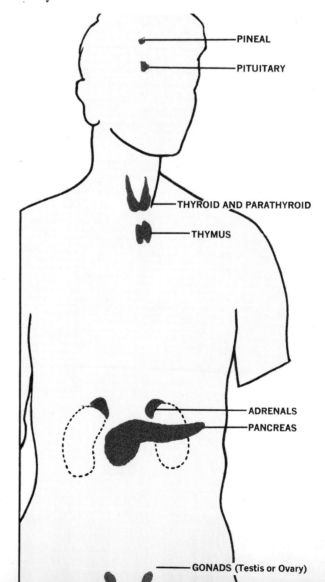

PINEAL

PITUITARY

THYROID AND PARATHYROID

THYMUS

ADRENALS

PANCREAS

GONADS (Testis or Ovary)

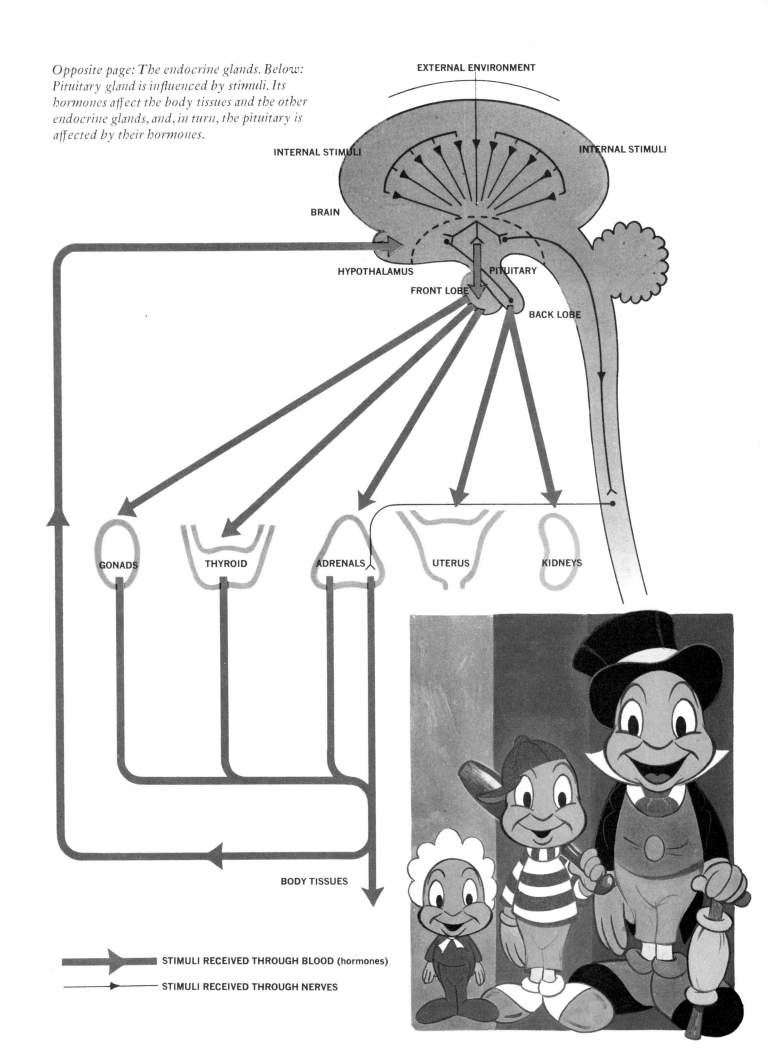

Opposite page: The endocrine glands. Below:
Pituitary gland is influenced by stimuli. Its
hormones affect the body tissues and the other
endocrine glands, and, in turn, the pituitary is
affected by their hormones.

EXTERNAL ENVIRONMENT

INTERNAL STIMULI

INTERNAL STIMULI

BRAIN

HYPOTHALAMUS

PITUITARY

FRONT LOBE

BACK LOBE

GONADS

THYROID

ADRENALS

UTERUS

KIDNEYS

BODY TISSUES

STIMULI RECEIVED THROUGH BLOOD (hormones)

STIMULI RECEIVED THROUGH NERVES

TYING EVERYTHING TOGETHER: THE ENDOCRINE SYSTEM

Somebody just asked me what part of the body we're going to explore next. I've been giving this some thought. You must forgive me if I don't tell you just yet. Trust your old friend Jiminy Cricket, and you'll soon see what I'm trying to do.

Let's leave our big, complex bodies, with their thousands of billions of cells, and talk a little while about the *protozoa*, a group of microscopic animals whose bodies are composed of just a single cell.

There is a large variety of these creatures. You may have seen some of them under the microscope. The one I have in mind is the ameba. It is a tiny, colorless blob of living material that lives in pond water. The ameba creeps along, or rather, it flows along. When it touches a bit of

food it just flows around the food, engulfing it. The ameba is a very primitive animal. But there is something you must understand, boys and girls. The ameba is every bit as alive as you are. The creature's life activities can be carried on more simply than yours because it is single-celled, and you are multi-celled. Let me explain what I mean.

Like the cells of your body, the ameba needs oxygen. The ameba's thin, skinlike cell membrane allows oxygen from the water to enter the cell. But most of your cells are buried deep in masses of tissue, thousands of cells in thickness. The only way these cells can get oxygen is to have it collected (by the respiratory system) and brought to them (by the circulatory system). Now, boys and girls, this holds true for other life activities, such as digestion and excretion. The ameba's single cell can take care of these activities, but we must have large, complex systems to do the work.

Now you'll see why I wanted to compare you with the ameba. The ameba can carry on all its life activities in a single cell. On the other hand, your large, complex organs are far apart. Let's take the excretory organs as an example, since we just finished talking about them. The kidneys, skin, lungs, and alimentary canal are all involved in the excretion of water. The amounts of water that need to be excreted from the body vary a great deal. They depend on the amount of water taken into the body, the kind of activities you are carrying on, the time of day, the temperature, the kind of food you ate, the state of your health, and other conditions. Can you imagine what would hap-

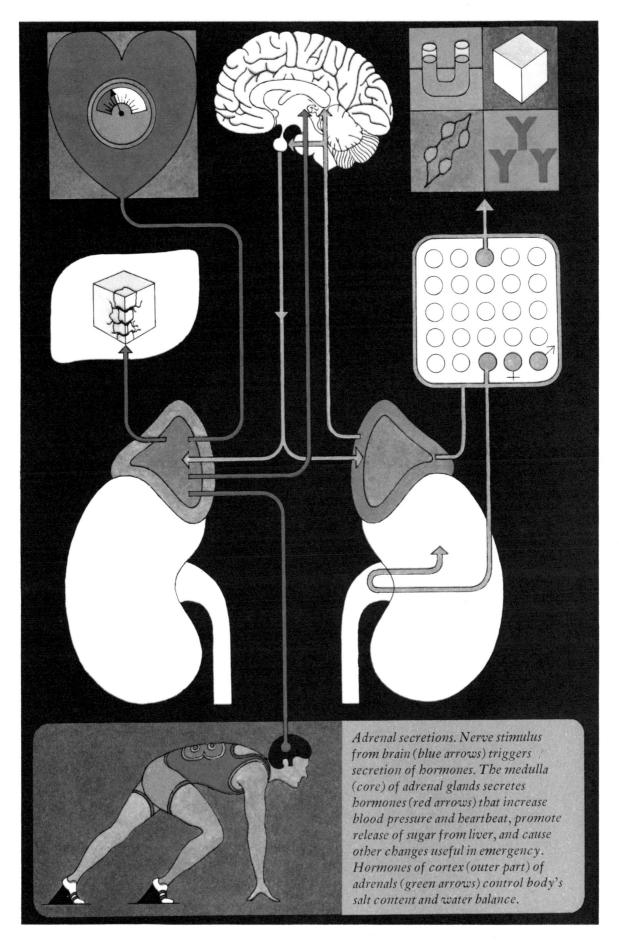

Adrenal secretions. Nerve stimulus from brain (blue arrows) triggers secretion of hormones. The medulla (core) of adrenal glands secretes hormones (red arrows) that increase blood pressure and heartbeat, promote release of sugar from liver, and cause other changes useful in emergency. Hormones of cortex (outer part) of adrenals (green arrows) control body's salt content and water balance.

pen if all these organs operated on their own? Some might excrete a lot, others very little. Or even worse, all of them might shut down at the same time! You can see we'd all be in very deep trouble rather quickly. What is it, Louie? Good for you, my boy! Louie says there has to be some kind of master control to tie the organs together, and to coordinate their activity.

There's really no need to look so worried boys and girls! Of course you all have a master control system. Otherwise you wouldn't have reached your advanced age. In fact—this is really very good news

—you have two master control systems, not just one. One of them—I've mentioned it before—is the *nervous system*. It coordinates the kind of activities that occur quickly. We'll go into the work of the nervous system later on. But now we'll take a good look at the work of the *endocrine system*, which controls mainly the activities that take place more slowly.

You've already met the kind of organs that make up the endocrine system. They are glands. Do you remember the digestive glands, such as those that secrete (make) digestive juices in the mouth and stomach? Those glands have tubes or ducts through which the juices flow into the mouth or stomach. But the glands in the endocrine system have no ducts—in fact, they are often called ductless glands. What's that, Huey? You want to know how the juices get out of the gland without a duct? I'm glad you asked that question, because I think you can answer it yourself, with a little hint from me. Do you know of any way in which liquids can move around to various parts of the body? Right! Through the circulatory system, of course!

Endocrine glands are very well supplied with blood vessels. As the gland secretes its particular chemicals, they are absorbed into the bloodstream and carried quickly by the blood to all parts of the body. For example, the secretions of the *adrenal glands*, which are attached to the top of the kidneys, reach the heart in seconds, causing it to pump a greater amount of blood.

Other endocrine glands work in the same general way, by sending their secretions into the blood. The secretions can affect organs at a distance in the body. The name given to these secretions is *hormones*. "Hormones" comes from a Greek word meaning "to arouse or stir

Opposite page: Front lobe of pituitary gland secretes a growth hormone. Too much of hormone is a cause of gigantism, while too little produces a dwarf. Above: White rats and other laboratory animals are used to study effects of hormones.

up," and you can see that it is really a very well-chosen name.

Endocrine glands and their hormones were not well understood until recently, and even today scientists are making many new discoveries about them. Well, my friends, we can't hope to make a deep study of this subject, but you might like to hear a few interesting things about the endocrines.

I already mentioned the adrenals, a pair of glands that together weigh about ½ ounce. Small as they are, the adrenals are actually two glands in one. *Cortin*, the hormone secreted by the outer part, or *cortex*, of the gland, controls water balance in the body. The inner part, or *medulla*, secretes a hormone that causes body changes that may be useful in an emergency.

Then there is the thyroid gland, which controls the rate at which the body cells burn food, and affects growth in young people.

Do you remember we talked about a digestive gland called the pancreas, which

69

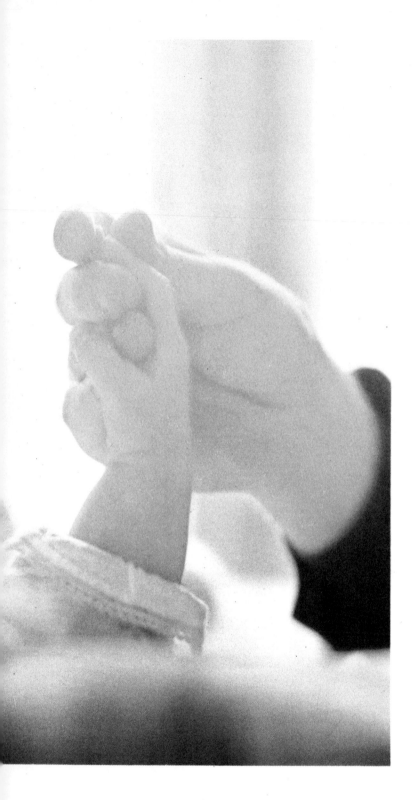

Above: The nervous system of a newborn child is already highly developed. It regulates vital activities such as breathing and heart action. It also controls automatic actions (reflexes) such as sucking and grasping. Right: The marvel of new life is communicated in the painting The Birth of the Virgin *by Boccaccio Boccaccino.*

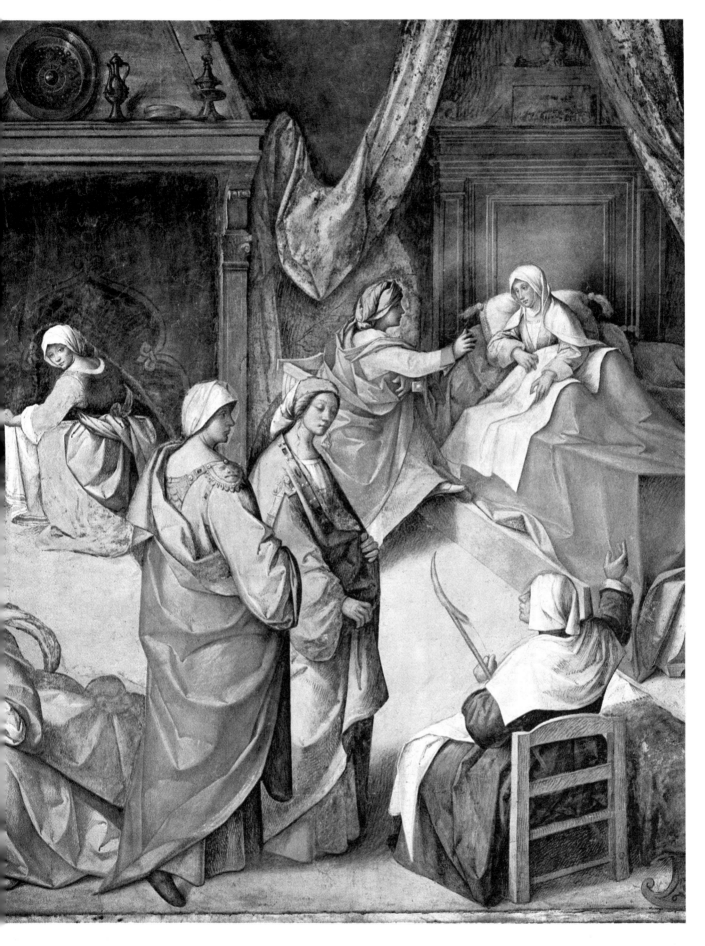

sends its juices into the small intestine? Well, the pancreas is a very special gland, because some parts of it are ductless. These parts secrete a hormone called *insulin*. This very important hormone controls the storage of sugar, and its use by the body cells. Lack of insulin causes the disease called *diabetes*. However, the thyroid, adrenals, and a gland called the *pituitary* are also involved.

The pituitary, which weighs about one fiftieth of an ounce, is located at the base of the brain. In spite of its tiny size, it is enormously important. It secretes many hormones, which influence many parts and glands of the body. Some of its hormones are concerned with growth and with the development of the sex organs. Other pituitary hormones stimulate the activity of the adrenal glands and the thyroid. Still other hormones regulate blood pressure and stimulate smooth (involuntary) muscles.

At one time the many activities of the pituitary led to its being called the "master gland." Today, however, scientists recognize that the pituitary not only gives orders to other glands, it also takes orders from them. And the other glands, my friends, include some that we haven't even mentioned—the pineal, thymus, parathyroids, and more. It all adds up to a complex system of chemical checks and balances that keep your body in order.

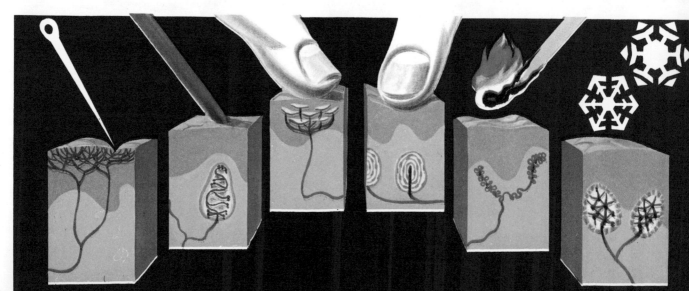

WINDOWS ON THE WORLD: THE SENSES

Boys and girls, I'd like all of you to sit down and make yourselves comfortable. We're going to do an experiment, but first I want you to think a bit. It will be a very short thinking session, I promise.

You've learned a lot (at least I hope you have) about the way your body

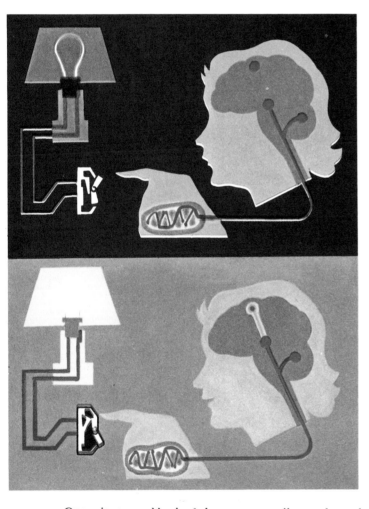

Opposite page: Much of the sense we call taste depends on another sense, the sense of smell. When you drink hot chocolate, for example, vapor from the drink, entering through the nostrils, reaches smell-sensing areas deep in the nasal cavities. At the same time, the taste is sensed by taste buds in the tongue.
Opposite page, bottom: Different kinds of nerve endings in skin react to pain, touch, pressure, heat, cold.
Left above: Like closing of a switch in electric circuit, contact of skin with object triggers stimulus to brain.
Right, above: Millions of nerve endings in skin of entire body report on our surroundings.

works. We've been thinking about you as though you were a small world of your own, with wonderful systems for taking in food, using it, excreting wastes, and doing all the many other things needed to be alive. But we should remember that you're not a world to yourself. You live in surroundings made up of people, buildings, rain, sounds, dangers to be avoided, and thousands of other things that you must be aware of.

Dewey, please stop squirming, we'll be finished with this heavy thinking in just another minute. To live, you must not only have your body systems working well, you must also be able to sense what is happening in your surroundings. How do you do that? Ah, Dewey wants to tell us. We have a sense of sight, and a sense of hearing. Very good, Dewey. Anything to add, Louie? Right you are—the senses of touch, taste, and smell.

Well, boys and girls, there we have the five senses—our windows on the world

People who have lost one or more of their senses can succeed in life. Perhaps the most famous case of a handicapped person who succeeded is that of Helen Keller, who was born a normal child in 1880. Before she was two, illness deprived her of her sight and hearing. Anne Sullivan, a special teacher, created a bond between Helen and the world through the little girl's sense of touch. Helen could "hear" Anne by placing her hand over her teacher's lips. She earned a college degree, became a writer, and was honored by famous people such as Alexander Graham Bell and Eleanor Roosevelt (above). She toured the world, giving hope to deaf and blind persons. Opposite page: A boy enjoying cotton candy. Which of his senses are involved here?

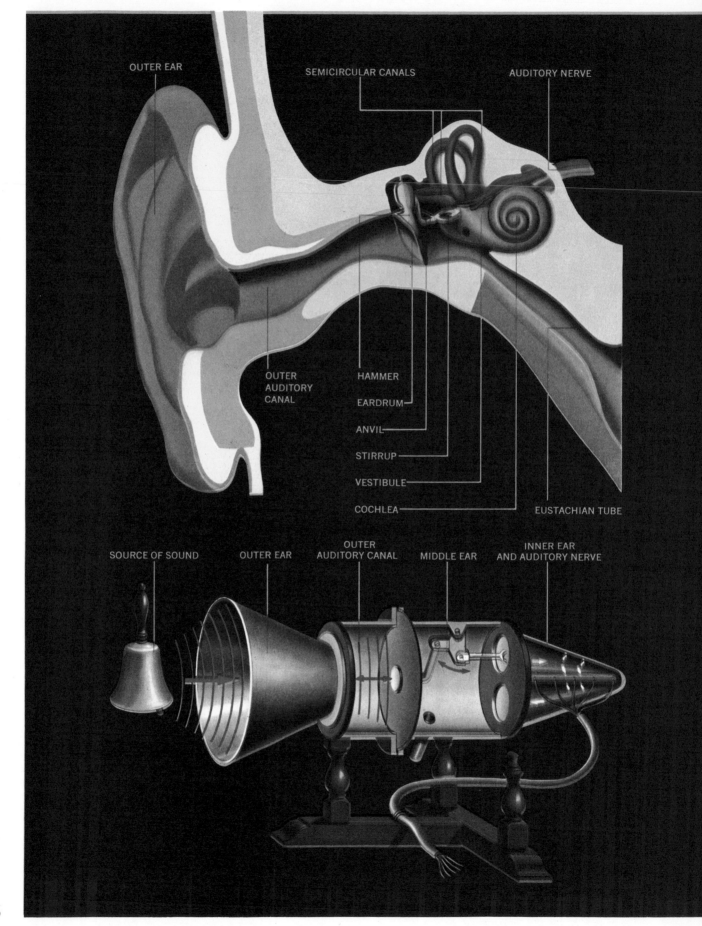

OUTER EAR

SEMICIRCULAR CANALS

AUDITORY NERVE

OUTER
AUDITORY
CANAL

HAMMER

EARDRUM

ANVIL

STIRRUP

VESTIBULE

COCHLEA

EUSTACHIAN TUBE

SOURCE OF SOUND

OUTER EAR

OUTER
AUDITORY CANAL

MIDDLE EAR

INNER EAR
AND AUDITORY NERVE

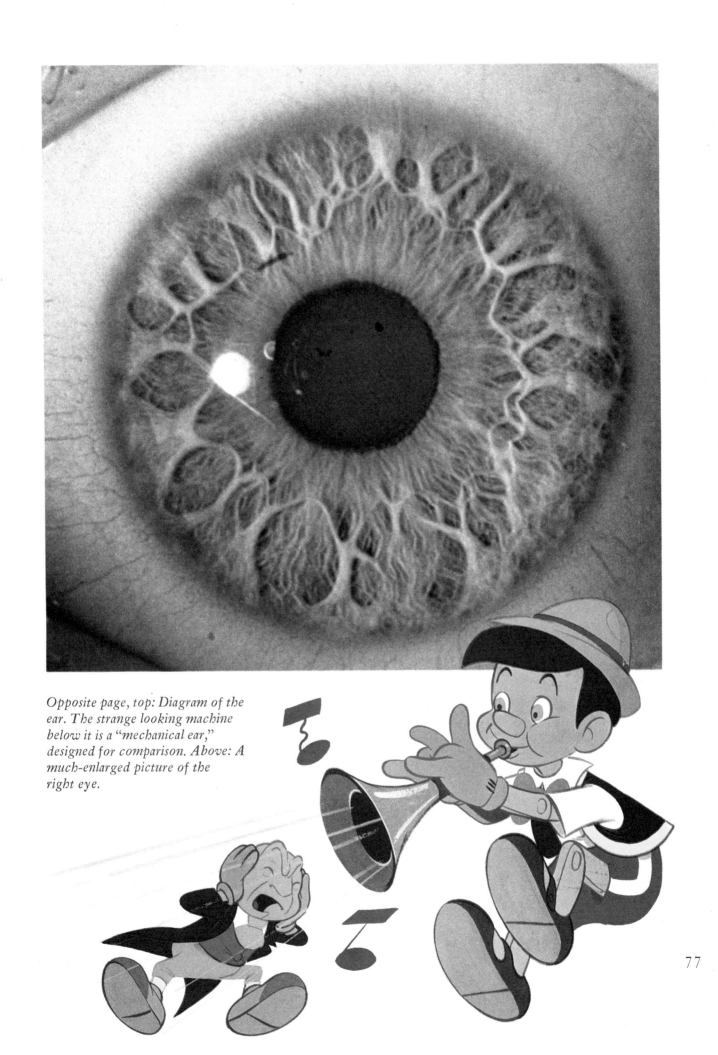

Opposite page, top: Diagram of the ear. The strange looking machine below it is a "mechanical ear," designed for comparison. Above: A much-enlarged picture of the right eye.

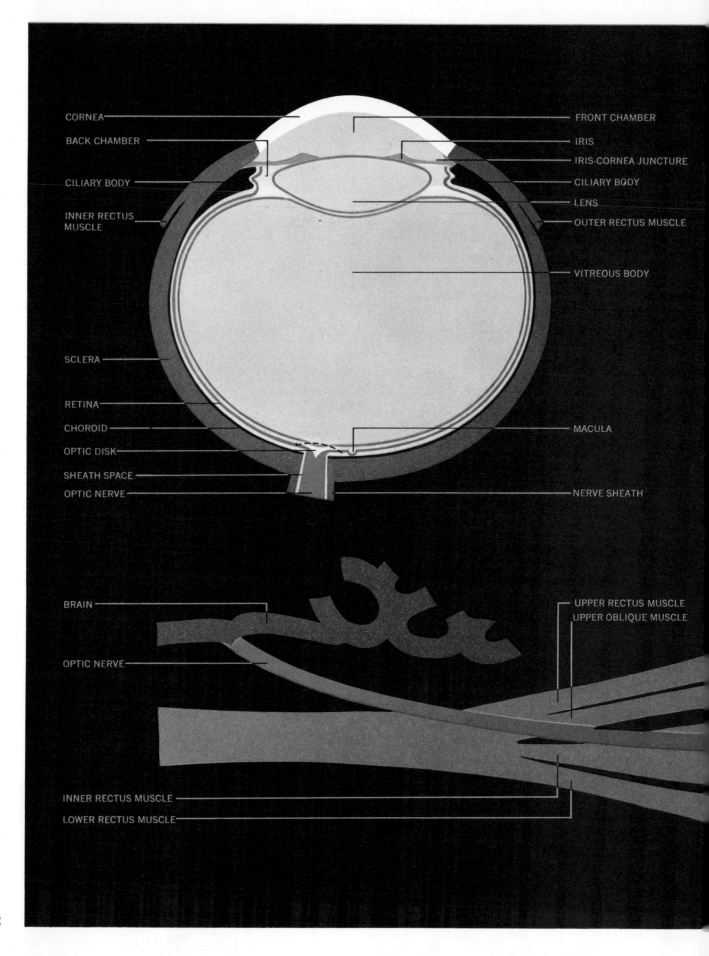

CORNEA

BACK CHAMBER

CILIARY BODY

INNER RECTUS
MUSCLE

SCLERA

RETINA

CHOROID

OPTIC DISK

SHEATH SPACE

OPTIC NERVE

FRONT CHAMBER

IRIS

IRIS-CORNEA JUNCTURE

CILIARY BODY

LENS

OUTER RECTUS MUSCLE

VITREOUS BODY

MACULA

NERVE SHEATH

BRAIN

OPTIC NERVE

UPPER RECTUS MUSCLE
UPPER OBLIQUE MUSCLE

INNER RECTUS MUSCLE

LOWER RECTUS MUSCLE

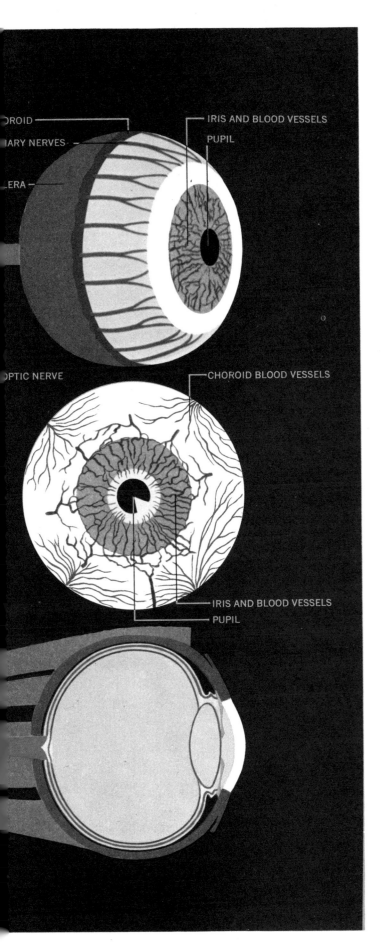

CROID

IARY NERVES

ERA

IRIS AND BLOOD VESSELS

PUPIL

PTIC NERVE

CHOROID BLOOD VESSELS

IRIS AND BLOOD VESSELS

PUPIL

around us. People always speak of the "five" senses, so it's easy to get the idea that there are only five. There are more. In a little while, for example, you will become aware that you are hungry or thirsty or uncomfortable. You need inside senses to report these conditions to you. Would you like to try a little experiment to test one of the inside senses? Listen carefully and follow my directions exactly.

Sit as you are, eyes closed. Move your arms about—any way you like. Not so fast, Huey, you'll hurt someone! Keep moving your arms until I tell you to stop. Then there is to be no motion at all. All right, stop! Don't move any more!

Can you tell (your eyes are still closed!) whether each arm is straight or bent? Near your body or out to one side? Pointed up or down? Wrists straight or bent? Palms facing up? Down? Fingers straight out? Bent? All right now, open your eyes. How many of you had the right answers? Of course, you all did! Now you've seen an inside sense at work. This one is *muscle sense*. Other inner senses report other facts to you, so you

Far left: A cross section of the eye. Top and center: The network of blood vessels in the eye. Bottom: Some of the muscles that move the eye.

are aware of what goes on inside you at all times.

Now I think we're ready to explore the five senses further. Let's begin with the sense of sight. That makes you think of the eye at once. This remarkable organ is very much like a camera. The *pupil*, an opening in the front of the eye, allows light reflected from objects to enter the eye. Look at your neighbor's eye, everybody. The pupil is the black circle at the center. The colored ring that surrounds the pupil is the *iris*. By narrowing or widening automatically in bright or dim light, the iris controls the amount of light that gets to the inside of the eye. A lens behind the pupil gathers the light, so a small image of the object is formed. In your camera, this image falls on the film. Of course, there is no film in the back of your eye. Instead, the image is received on the *retina*, a sort of screen. The retina

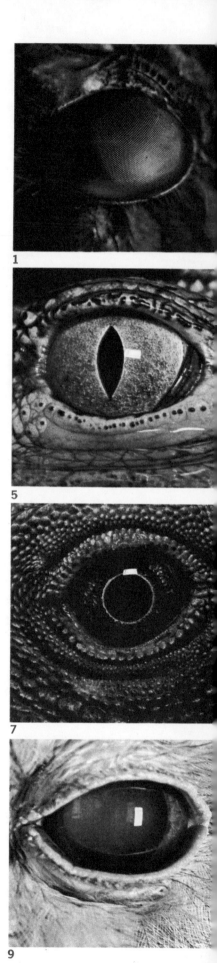

1

5

7

9

80

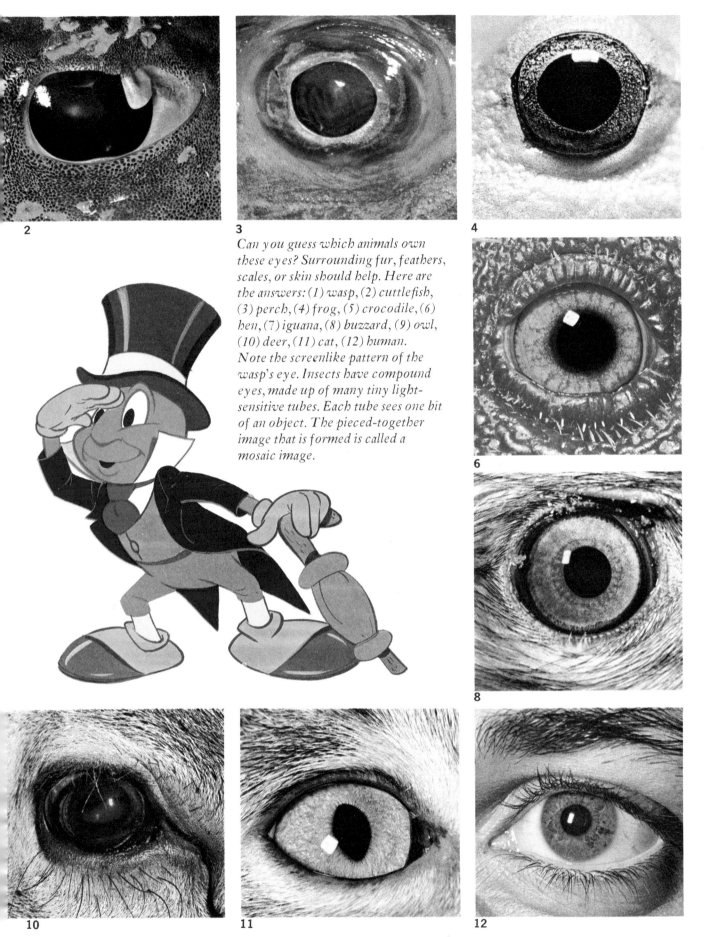

2

3

4

Can you guess which animals own these eyes? Surrounding fur, feathers, scales, or skin should help. Here are the answers: (1) wasp, (2) cuttlefish, (3) perch, (4) frog, (5) crocodile, (6) hen, (7) iguana, (8) buzzard, (9) owl, (10) deer, (11) cat, (12) human. Note the screenlike pattern of the wasp's eye. Insects have compound eyes, made up of many tiny light-sensitive tubes. Each tube sees one bit of an object. The pieced-together image that is formed is called a mosaic image.

6

8

10

11

12

is lined with nerve cells that are sensitive to light. These cells send impulses (messages) to the brain, and you see as a result.

Girls and boys, there is a very important point here that must be understood. The eye is a wonderfully made organ, but it sees nothing. It is only a reporter that sends messages to the brain. The actual seeing occurs in the brain. As we go on to talk about the other senses you should remember that hearing, tasting, and so on do not take place in the ear or tongue, but in the brain.

Well, is everybody ready for the sense of hearing? Good! You hear because your ears can detect vibrations. Every sound causes vibrations, usually in the air. These vibrations are *sound waves*. The opening into your ear leads to a thin sheet of tightly stretched tissue, the *eardrum*. The eardrum vibrates when the sound waves strike it, and it passes the vibrations along to a set of three tiny bones. These tiny bones in turn pass the vibrations to a snail-shaped liquid-filled chamber, the *cochlea*. Here nerve cells sense the vibrations. They send impulses to the brain, and you hear.

Your ear is one of those two-in-one organs like some we've seen before. It serves for more than hearing. In each inner ear, near the cochlea, there is a set of three ringlike hollow tubes, the *semicircular canals*. Each canal lies in a different plane. You will see what I mean if you can imagine that one of the canals lies on the seat of a chair, the second is flat against the back of the chair, and the third lies flat against the arm of the chair. There is liquid in the canals, and if your head moves ever so slightly, the liquid moves in one or more of the canals. Nerve cells in the canals send impulses to the brain, so you are always kept aware of your position. Yes, Huey, I'm glad you

recognized it. It is your sense of balance.

Now we're coming to one of your favorite senses, the one that lets you enjoy the flavors of all the things you like best. It's the sense of taste, of course. As you know, the tongue reports on taste. But you may not know that different parts of the tongue sense different tastes. Sweet things, for example, are tasted chiefly at the front of the tongue, while sour tastes are felt at the sides. Actually, taste depends a great deal on the sense of smell. When you have a cold and your nose is stuffed, you can neither smell nor taste anything.

Taste and smell are both chemical senses. They depend on a chemical reaction between the substance and the cells that do the sensing.

Well, let me see, what have we left out? Oh, of course, the senses of touch. No, Louie, that wasn't a mistake, I meant to say senses. There are several senses of touch, not just one. For example, you can tell by touching, the difference between this page and a piece of cloth. You might call that a sense of texture. You can also feel the pressure of a hand on your shoulder or the temperature of the water you swim in by their effects on nerve endings in the skin. It would be nice if we could spend more time on the senses. But we must go on to the computerlike organ that feels, learns, remembers, and controls —the brain.

Figure 1

Figure 2

Figure 3

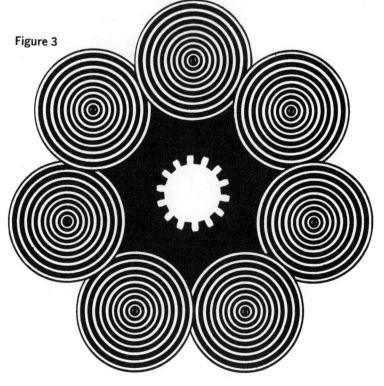

Sometimes the brain, using its past experience, interprets wrongly what the eyes report. These drawings create such optical illusions. Fig. 1: The ropelike character of the concentric circles makes them seem to spiral. Fig. 2: The star seems to flash. Fig. 3: Turn the book one way, and the wheels seem to turn in the opposite direction. Fig. 4: The parallel horizontal lines seem to bend inward at left, outward at right. Opposite page: Colored dots are test of color perception. If you see colors perfectly, you will see 29 in "a," 45 in "b," 26 in "d," and no number in "c."

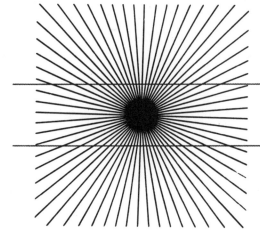

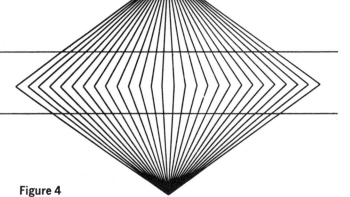

Figure 4

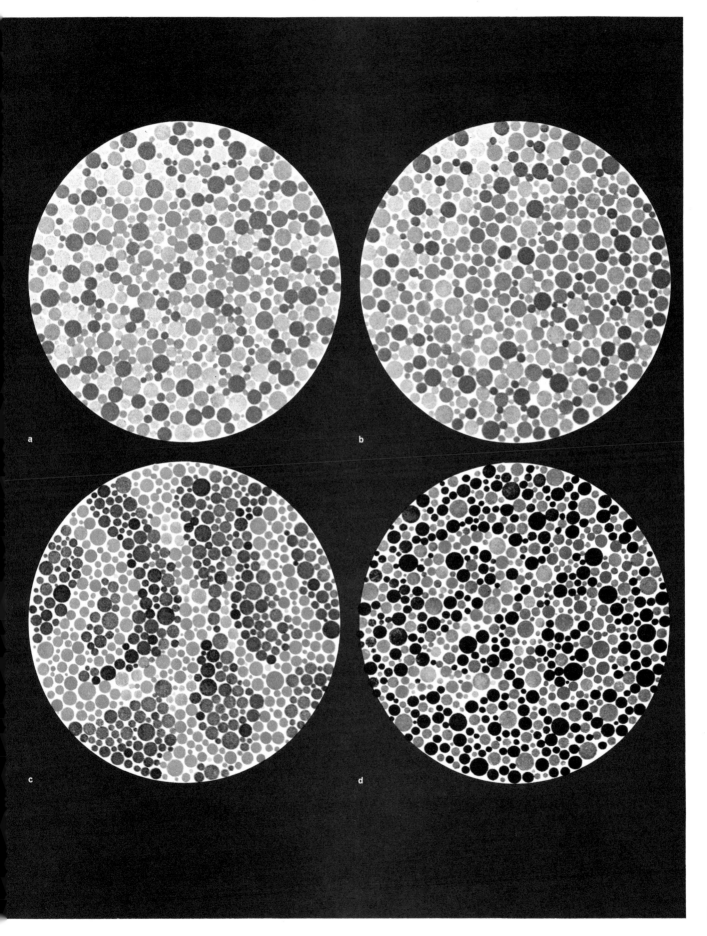

TYING EVERYTHING TOGETHER: THE BRAIN

Our long journey has finally brought us to the brain, the center of the nervous system. It is an organ whose work is enormously complicated. In trying to describe what the brain does, people sometimes compare it to a busy telephone switchboard, with thousands of messages arriving and going out every minute. This is a very good comparison. Sometimes the brain is compared to a computer. That's a good comparison, too, for the brain does many things computers do. It also does things computers can't do—or at least, not yet.

Huey wants to know how we can understand anything about the brain if it is so complex. Well, boys and girls, *how* the brain works is still very much of a mystery. *What* it does, however, is better known, and it isn't hard to understand. So just lend an ear to your good friend, Jiminy Cricket, and learn.

Let's go back to the senses for a moment. We said that the eyes don't really see. They sense light and report what they sense by sending signals, or impulses, to the brain. The brain interprets the impulses as the face of a friend, a dish of ice cream, or a page of this book. The other senses, hearing, taste, and so on, are similarly felt, not by the sense organ, but are interpreted by the brain.

The brain is the control center of the body. It is surrounded by the immovable bones of the skull, which form a space called the cranial cavity. This affords maximum protection for the brain. Communication between the brain and the rest of the body is carried on by nerves, most of which lie in the spinal cord, and branch out from it to all parts of the body. Opposite page: A. Color key shows the main sections of lobes of the brain. 1: frontal lobe; 2: parietal lobe; 3: temporal lobe; 4: occipital lobe; 5: cerebellum. Lobes 1 through 4 are part of the cerebrum, which is very highly developed in man. The cerebrum controls intelligent activity, the senses, will, and motion. The cerebellum coordinates muscular movements. For example, throwing a ball involves dozens of muscles in the arms and trunk. Each muscle must do its bit at exactly the right time. In addition, the cerebellum helps to keep the balance of the body. B. Colored dots indicate control centers for particular areas of the body. 1: vision; 2: sensation and movement of arms; 3: sensation and movement of legs; 4: language centers; 5: sensation and movement of face; 6: sensation and movement of tongue. C. Folded pattern of brain surface (convolutions) allows room for more surface area in same amount of space in cranial cavity. Wood figure shows position of brain within head.

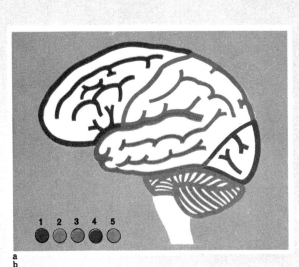

a

b

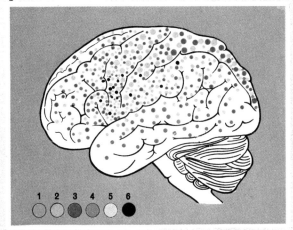

c

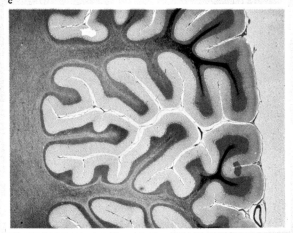

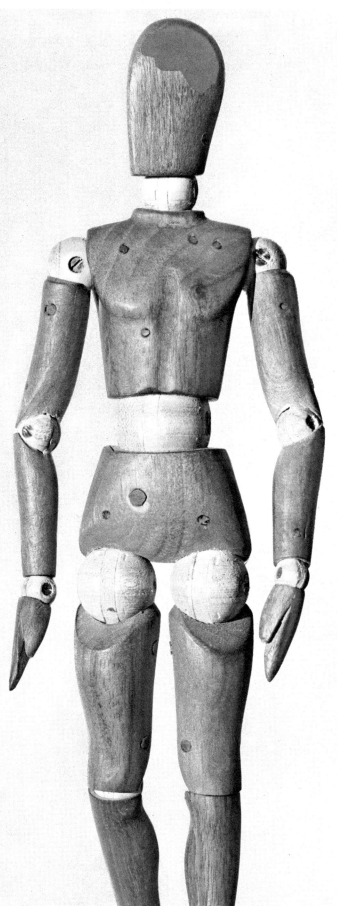

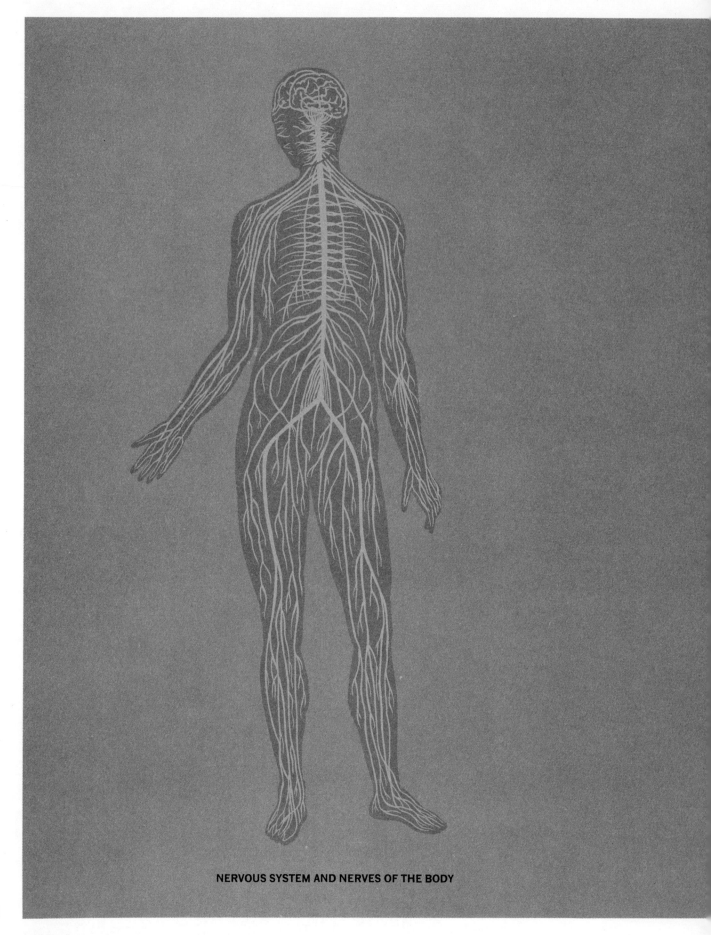

NERVOUS SYSTEM AND NERVES OF THE BODY

Just imagine the enormous number of impulses that pour into the brain every second! Suppose you are standing at the curb, waiting to cross the street. People are walking toward you and away from you. They are men, women, boys and girls, tall, short, thin and fat, smiling and scowling, alone, in pairs, or in groups, carrying books or bags, wearing hats or bare-headed. Automobiles are moving or standing. All sorts of sounds are heard. Your sensory system senses all of these facts, and many more, continuously reporting them all to the brain.

Yes, Louie, the brain must indeed be a busy place, but I assure you we are only at the beginning of its activities. Much more is needed than just to be aware of what is happening around you. The brain must coordinate all the impulses it receives, for they come from different sensory organs. And the brain must separate instantly what is important from all the rest. For example, at this moment, the color of the traffic light and sight of moving cars is important. A few seconds

Opposite page: The human nervous system includes the central nervous system (that is, the brain and spinal cord) and the peripheral (outer) nervous system, which is connected to the central system and controlled by it. The peripheral system is also connected to skeletal (body) muscles, receptors such as the eye and ear, and involuntary muscles such as those in the digestive system.

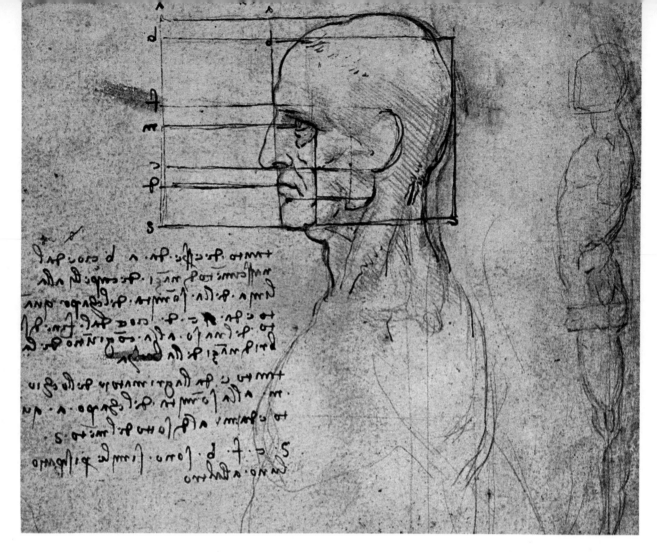

The skull cavity protects the brain within. The arched roof of the skull, like the arched roof of the stadium on the opposite page, resists downward pressures or blows. The drawing of the skull, above, is the work of the great Italian artist and scientist, Leonardo da Vinci.

later, after you have crossed safely, recognizing a face coming toward you may be more important.

Once the brain has weighed the facts, it makes its decision. It sends impulses to the muscles of the legs and trunk to act, so you walk across the street.

Boys and girls, telling you this took me quite a while. The brain takes only a very tiny fraction of a second to receive the impulses, coordinate them, sort out the important from the unimportant, make a decision, and send out the needed orders.

Does it seem to you that the brain is without doubt the most amazing of all the amazing organs we've discussed? Of course it is. Looking at the brain wouldn't give you the least clue to how it can do all the wonderful things it does. But under the microscope, a small bit of brain tissue, colored with a special dye, has something to tell. We can see *neurons*, the type of cells that make up the brain. Each cell is shaped like a pyramid. Short thread-like branches, called *dendrites*, extend from each corner of the pyramid.

Your brain, Huey (yours too, Louie and Dewey), contains about 10,000,000,-000 (billion) of these cells. But billions of additional neurons are found throughout your body, making up all the nerves. Neurons vary with the job they do. Some, like those in the brain, have only short dendrites. Others, in addition to the dendrites, have a long fiber called an *axon*. The axons of some neurons are 2 feet or more long! Still other neurons are of the specialized kind found in various

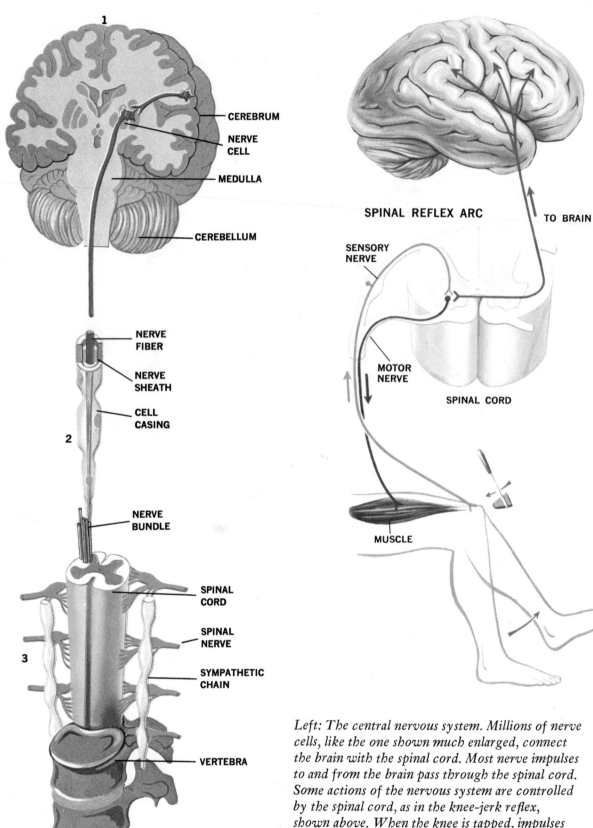

1

CEREBRUM

NERVE CELL

MEDULLA

CEREBELLUM

2

NERVE FIBER

NERVE SHEATH

CELL CASING

NERVE BUNDLE

3

SPINAL CORD

SPINAL NERVE

SYMPATHETIC CHAIN

VERTEBRA

SPINAL REFLEX ARC

TO BRAIN

SENSORY NERVE

MOTOR NERVE

SPINAL CORD

MUSCLE

Left: The central nervous system. Millions of nerve cells, like the one shown much enlarged, connect the brain with the spinal cord. Most nerve impulses to and from the brain pass through the spinal cord. Some actions of the nervous system are controlled by the spinal cord, as in the knee-jerk reflex, shown above. When the knee is tapped, impulses flash from the knee to the spinal cord. Other impulses, from the spinal cord to the leg muscles, cause the muscles to contract, and the leg jumps suddenly. The brain receives the information, but by that time the action, or reflex, has occurred.

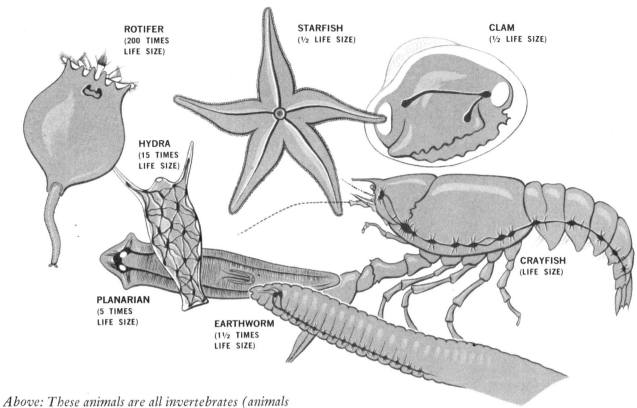

ROTIFER
(200 TIMES
LIFE SIZE)

STARFISH
(½ LIFE SIZE)

CLAM
(½ LIFE SIZE)

HYDRA
(15 TIMES
LIFE SIZE)

CRAYFISH
(LIFE SIZE)

PLANARIAN
(5 TIMES
LIFE SIZE)

EARTHWORM
(1½ TIMES
LIFE SIZE)

*Above: These animals are all invertebrates (animals
without spines). Their simple nervous systems,
shown in color, can receive information and react to
it. However, they do not have complex brains
like those of the vertebrates (animals with spines).
Below: Brains of vertebrates. In the more
complex animals, the cerebrum is generally large
compared to the rest of the brain.*

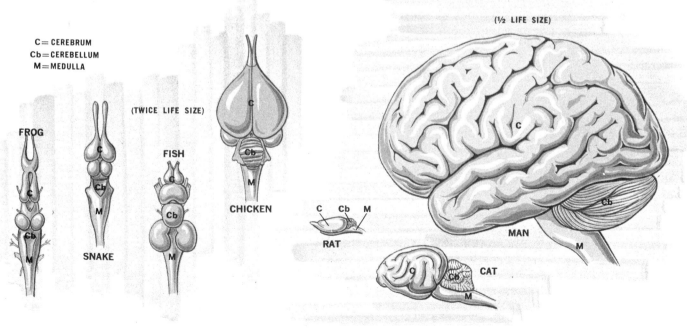

C = CEREBRUM
Cb = CEREBELLUM
M = MEDULLA

FROG

SNAKE

(TWICE LIFE SIZE)

FISH

CHICKEN

RAT

(½ LIFE SIZE)

MAN

CAT

sense organs, able to sense heat, light, sound, or some other condition of our surroundings.

What's that, Louie? You want to know what the neurons do? Well, let's keep in mind that the nervous system depends on the movement of impulses through the system at very high speeds. Neurons are fitted for this kind of communication. They can produce signals that are actually very short bursts of electricity. These tiny currents are the impulses we've spoken about. A neuron receives an impulse through its dendrites from a neighboring neuron. It sets up another impulse, which passes through the axon to still another neuron. One neuron

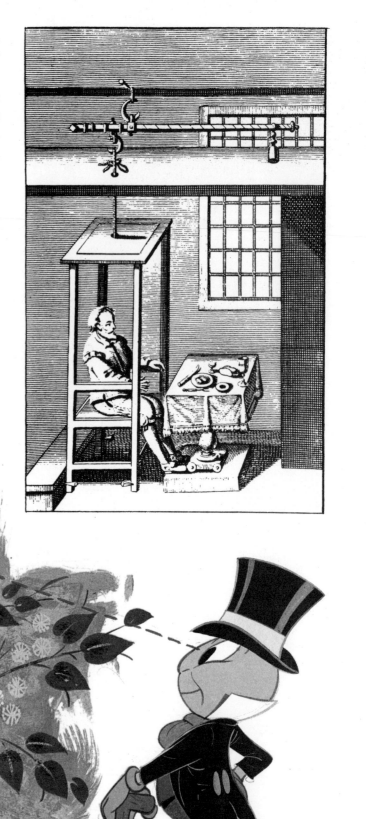

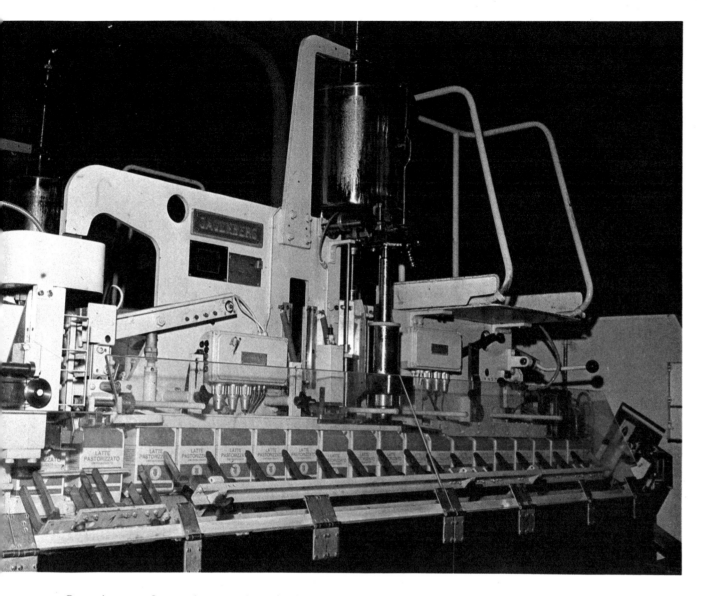

Opposite page: Sanctorius, an Italian physician, lived in a "scale room," weighing all his food and wastes, to learn how the body uses food. A part of our food (for example, proteins and minerals in the milk being bottled in the photograph above) becomes part of the living material in our body cells.

can send along hundreds of impulses in a single second!

The impulses travel at speeds of up to several hundred miles per hour, so an impulse can go from your head to your foot in just a very small fraction of a second.

Well now, I was going to tell you about the brain, but all I've done so far is lead you up to it. Let's get right to it. The brain is located inside the head, of course. It weighs a little over 3 pounds in an adult, and it is the organ that senses, makes connections, and issues the orders that control all the body organs.

The brain is well protected, as we might expect for an organ so important. The bony skull surrounds it, and, in addition, several tough membranes and a layer of liquid cushion the brain against shock.

The outside of the brain is full of wrinkles, called *convolutions*. They increase the area of the outer surface of the brain, so a greater number of nerve cells can exist in the same amount of space within the skull cavity.

By far the largest part of your brain is the *cerebrum*. This part of the brain is concerned with intelligent activity. Particular areas of the cerebrum are connected with particular activities. For example, the sense of sight is concentrated at the back of the cerebrum, the upper central portion controls movements of the organs of the body, and the front areas are concerned with thinking activity.

We don't have the time to go into all the parts of the brain, but one part you really should know about is the *cerebellum*. Its work helps you to keep your balance and to make coordinated movements. Another small but vital part of the brain is the *medulla*. It is vital because

A roomful of computer equipment. Computers do much of the time-consuming comparing and calculating that is needed in scientific work, giving scientists more time for their research work.

the medulla controls both the heartbeat and breathing automatically.

And "automatic" reminds me, dear friends, that I must mention the spinal cord, which controls certain reflex actions. These are actions not under your control. When you touch a hot object, for example, your spinal cord, acting like an assistant brain, orders the muscles to pull the hand away. The act occurs even before you are aware of the danger. Precious hundredths of a second are saved in such a dangerous situation.

AUTOMATIC ACTION IN THE BODY

Is everybody here and ready to listen? Huey, I'm sure you'll find it easier to concentrate if you put away that basketball. I think you must all realize by now that you are remarkably advanced, highly intelligent creatures. No, Dewey, I certainly am not joking! Human beings like yourself have devised jet planes and space probes, developed vaccines against deadly diseases, and written great poetry. No other animal can do any of these things because no other animal has your highly developed cerebrum, with its ability to think, remember, compare, judge, and imagine.

Well, now that I've convinced you of the greatness of your brain, you'll be surprised to hear that most of the activities controlled by your brain are automatic. These kinds of activities your pet cat can perform as well as you can. Let's have a look at some of these activities.

I'll begin by telling you about a very pleasant thing that happened yesterday. What a beautiful day it was! Well, boys and girls, I was strolling in the park, and I stopped to admire a bird in a tree. It chirped once or twice, then broke into full, rich song. It stopped, then it repeated the song, over and over. My friends, I can't tell you how moved I was! I just had to sit down, take pencil and paper from my pocket, and write a little poem about the day, the bird, and its beautiful song, That poem was a real little masterpiece, I tell you!

Well, no, Louie, I don't happen to have the poem with me. What was that, Huey? Oh, you want to know what all this has to do with automatic activity. A great deal, really, as you'll see when I've finished.

Now, boys and girls, I'm sure that you'll agree that writing a little masterpiece calls for great intelligence, deep thought, imagination, and so on. None of that automatic activity here, eh? But that poem could never have been written without a lot of automatic activity, and here's why.

As I sat there writing I had to breathe, of course, and my heart had to go on beating. But those things didn't bother me. My medulla took charge of those activities, as it always does, leaving my cerebrum free to admire the beauties of nature. Other parts of my nervous system took care of directing activities such as digesting my breakfast, stimulating the sweat glands as the day grew warmer, supplying my body cells with nutrients, controlling the amount of light entering my eyes, and sitting upright without falling over.

That's a lot of automatic activity, but it isn't all. Even the writing of the poem

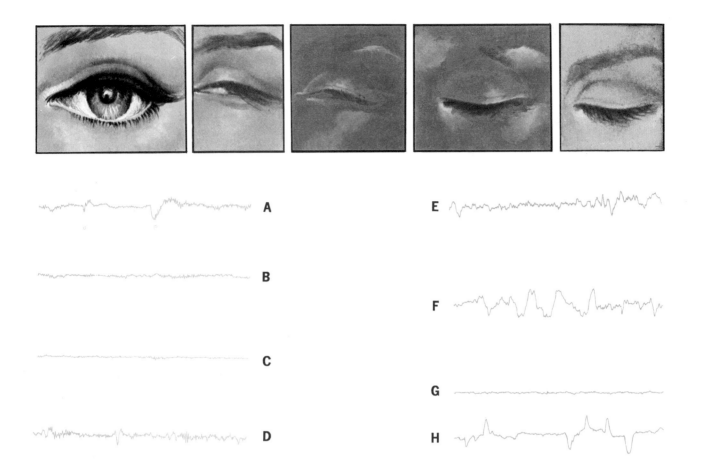

A

E

B

F

C

G

D

H

Above: Brain-wave tracings. The tracing at A was made by a subject who was awake but drowsy. Tracing B was made at the beginning of sleep; and C, D, and E followed as the sleep deepened. F was the point of deepest sleep, followed by G. The pattern at H is a record of eye movements during sleep. During periods of dreaming the eyes move rapidly behind the closed eyelids.

was partly automatic. My hand wrote without my having to think about moving it, and the spelling of the words came without thought. Now, children, could I have written that poem without automatic activities? Oh, it was my masterpiece, to be sure, but you must admit I had a lot of help!

Boys and girls, I think this may be a good time to point out to you that the things I talk about weren't learned quickly or easily. Thousands of great minds, working over many centuries, discovered the things we talk about casually. Today, in laboratories all over the world, scientists are searching for even more knowledge about our bodies. So much is known today that nobody can expect

to be an expert in everything. You will find that the study of the body is not one science, but many. Now that you know something about the body, I think you'll be interested in hearing what some of these sciences are about.

Anatomy is probably the oldest of the studies of the human body. The word comes from Greek words that mean "to cut up," for that was what the early researchers did with dead bodies. Many of them got into serious trouble, for the body was believed to be sacred. Oh yes, don't let me forget to tell you! Anatomy is the study of the parts of the body.

By the way, boys and girls, I don't want you to get the idea that these sciences are limited to human beings, or

99

even to animals. There are scientists, for example, who are specialists in plant anatomy.

The early researchers studied only what could be seen with the unaided eye. This is the science of *Gross Anatomy*. After the invention of the microscope, new kinds of anatomical studies developed. There was *Cytology*, for example, the study of cells. Another microscopic science is *Histology*, the study of tissues such as bone, blood, and muscle. Histology is sometimes called by the more descriptive name of *Microscopic Anatomy*.

It wasn't very long before scientists recognized that many mysteries about parts of the body could be answered by studying the way the body develops before birth. The new science that came into being was called *Embryology*.

Now, children, the sciences I've mentioned are concerned mainly with the *structure* of the body—that is, the way it is made. Other scientists became interested in the *functions* of the body—that is, the way that the body works. This is the science of *Physiology*. And, as more and more was learned, special branches of physiology began to appear.

One of these branches is *Biochemistry*, a science in which a great deal of fascinating research is being done today. This science is concerned with the chemical reactions that go on in living things.

Nutrition is a science that relates to the way food is taken in and used by the body. I think you can see that it is closely connected with biochemistry.

If you are going to be a doctor or a nurse you will have to learn a great deal about the normal body. But there is a science that is especially concerned with the changes that take place in the body when it is not in normal good health. This science is *Pathology*.

Well, boys and girls, I think I've said enough on this subject. But keep in mind that the sciences I've mentioned are only a few out of a great number, all concerned with probing deeper and deeper into the mysteries of the body.

THE MYSTERY OF SLEEP

Well, boys and girls, I hope that you are all feeling especially wide awake, because our topic is going to be—sleep. You may think it strange, boys and girls, that anything as ordinary as sleep should be a great mystery, but it is. For example, the cause of sleep—the reason why we fall asleep or stay awake—is not known for certain, although there are several theories about it.

But lots of things about sleep are known, and I'd like to tell you about some of them. People must have sleep. Without sleep they become irritable and lose the ability to think clearly or give full attention to their work. Scientists who have studied sleeping people tell us that most of the body's waking activities go on during sleep, but at a reduced rate. The heart beats more slowly, for example, the blood pressure is lowered, and the breathing is slower and deeper.

During sleep, your body temperature may fall 1 or 2 degrees. The body feels cooler when this happens. That explains why most people feel more comfortable with a cover, even if the night is not cold. Scientists made an interesting discovery

about the drop in body temperature. They learned that people who normally sleep at night have a temperature drop at night, even if they remain awake. Night workers who normally sleep during the day have their temperature drop during the day, even if they do not go to sleep. It is as if we had built-in clocks to regulate our body temperatures.

Well, you can see that it isn't too difficult to measure the heartbeat rate or the blood pressure of a sleeping person. But other questions about sleep were much harder to investigate, until the invention of a machine with the long name of *electroencephalograph*. It means "brain writing by electrical means." We'll have to understand the machine before we can understand how scientists learned from it.

Activity in the body is accompanied by the production of tiny electrical currents. You remember, for example, that such currents form the nerve impulses in communication between nerve cells. Another example is found in the heart, where each beat is accompanied by a set of currents.

In fact, a machine called the *electrocardiograph* (heart writing by electrical means) is used by doctors to detect and study the currents. An expert can tell a great deal about the health of the heart by analyzing the currents.

Well, boys and girls, your brains produce electric currents, too. No, Huey, they're far too weak to run any appliances. Extremely sensitive instruments, such as the electroencephalograph (EEG) are needed to detect the currents, or *brain waves*, as they are often called.

The EEG has a number of wires with *electrodes* (contacts) that are attached to the head of the person whose brain waves are to be studied. The currents from various parts of the brain reach the machine and are strengthened. This enables the currents to move a special set of pens. The pens move back and forth across a strip of moving paper, leaving a wavelike record of the currents that originated in the brain.

The waves are complex, and it takes long training and experience to analyze

Opposite page: Watch out! A car races through a red light, and your body's defenses are ready instantly.

102

them. But the experts know that particular wave patterns are connected with particular activities. Your waking waves differ according to your activities, and waking waves differ from sleeping waves. The waves of light sleep differ from those of deep sleep, and the waves of dreaming sleep differ from those of sleep without dreams.

Do you see how scientists can tell what is happening within your brain as you sleep? With the help of the EEG, they found that a night's sleep is made up of several cycles, each cycle lasting from 1½ to 2 hours. Each cycle includes some

Above: Scientists have found that excessive noise can affect hearing and mental health. In today's cities, automobiles, buses, and trucks pollute the air, not only with chemicals but also with noise. Jet planes taking off and landing add their screaming sounds, and supersonic transports will fill the air with their thunderous, frightening sonic booms. Industrial and construction activities add to the noises that surround us.

deep and some light sleep and—this will surprise you—each cycle ends with 5 to 10 minutes of dreaming. That means you may dream a total of more than an hour every night. Yes, Dewey, you do a lot of dreaming—we all do. But we forget nearly all of the dreams before we awake.

Many things about sleep are still un-known, and one of them is the answer to the question, "How much sleep is enough?" The amounts vary a good deal. Most adults need 7 to 9 hours of sleep daily, and about 10 hours should be the rule for a 12 year old. But remember, boys and girls, these are average hours of sleep.

COUNTER ATTACK!—THE BODY'S DEFENSES

Good morning, everybody, I hope you all slept the right number of hours last night. I'd like to tell you about some of the ways in which the body defends itself against its enemies.

Dewey wants to know what kind of enemies I mean. Well, Dewey, our surroundings are full of problems and dangers for the body. Wind, rain, cold, and heat can all be dangerous. Then there are cuts, scratches, bruises, and other injuries, all with dangerous possibilities for the body. And, of course, there are the most powerful enemies of all, the microscopic disease germs.

You know, this list would be very discouraging if our bodies didn't have a great arsenal of weapons for self-defense. These weapons are as varied as—well, as varied as the enemies that attack us.

Is it a very hot day? Blood vessels and sweat glands in your skin work together to keep your temperature steady, so your body will not become dangerously overheated. Is it cold and windy? Tiny muscles in your skin pull the pores tightly shut (that's the cause of "goose pimples"), to prevent loss of heat from the body.

Are you in danger? Perhaps a speeding car swings dangerously close to you, or you think you are being followed. At once, your adrenal glands send their hormone racing through the circulatory

A little boy's first snow. Good health habits and medical care will assure him of many more snows in the future.

system. Blood pressure and heartbeat rate increase, extra stored food from the liver pours into the blood, and the body muscles tighten up. All these changes could be useful if you had to stand and defend yourself, or if you had to run away quickly.

Boys and girls, is there anyone here who hasn't had a cut or scratch recently? Of course not! It's almost impossible to work and play actively without minor injuries, even if you're very careful. Yet loss of blood from even the smallest cut would be fatal without your blood clotting defense. The clotting process begins when platelets in the blood break up as they come in contact with the wound. The broken platelets release a chemical that triggers a long series of chemical reactions. The end result is the formation of a solid material that traps the blood cells like fish in a net, stopping the flow of blood.

The clot is only one part of the defense. Your skin is always covered with bacteria (germs). Of course there aren't quite so many germs, if you wash as often as you should. The bacteria are not a threat to you, as long as the skin remains unbroken. But some bacteria can be dangerous if they get into the body tissues through a break in the skin. Your defenses at this stage include the army of white blood cells that patrol the body constantly. White blood cells by the millions swarm into the injured area, surrounding, swallowing, and digesting the bacteria.

What's that, Louie? Yes, it really is a war between the body and the bacteria. Like real armies, the armies of the body use a variety of weapons and methods. You must realize that the skin itself is part of the war, like a fortress holding off an invader. We've already seen what happens when the fortress is invaded, as in a cut.

107

Well, good for you, Dewey! That was a fine question. He wants to know how we can keep bacteria from getting into the body along with food and air. Bacteria do enter the body and that calls for still another kind of defense. First, the lining of your digestive and respiratory systems contains cells that secrete *mucus*, a sticky fluid that traps many of the bacteria. Other lining cells sweep the mass of fluid and bacteria upward, to be discharged from the nose and mouth. Do you see now why you produce so much mucus when you have a cold? Bacteria that get into the body with food face a special defense in the stomach, which secretes an acid strong enough to kill the invaders.

Really now, isn't this array of defenses amazing? And that isn't all. Even if skin, mucus, acid, and white blood cells all fail, the inner defense, perhaps the most remarkable of all, may take over. It is *immunity*, the power to overcome a particular disease. We are all born with im-

munity to certain diseases, such as distemper, a dangerous disease of dogs.

During our lifetimes we develop immunity to certain diseases by having the disease or by having the germs of the disease in the body, without actually being ill. Either way, the body produces *antibodies* against that particular disease. Antibodies are chemicals that act against the germs causing the disease, or against the poisons (toxins) produced by the germs. This means that you don't get the disease a second time.

Another way to develop immunity is to be vaccinated. Weakened disease germs are injected into the body. The germs are too weak to make you sick, but they do cause your body to produce antibodies against that disease. In this way you develop immunity.

Opposite page: This lucky youngster is off to a fine start, with proper nutrition, good care, and the chance to play in the fresh air and sunlight.

CARING FOR THE MARVELOUS MACHINE

Boys and girls, we are coming to the end of our look at the human body. I've tried to help you to learn about the parts of this marvelous machine and how they work. When you buy a car, you are given a booklet. It tells you how to take care of the car, so it will run well and last a long time. This chapter will be such a booklet. We will discuss instructions for the care of a complicated, marvelous machine—you. The aim is a you that will be healthy and live a long time.

Our look at the body began with a look at its covering, the skin. Let's give the skin the place of honor again, as we learn to care for it. Being on the outside, the skin gets dirty, so it must be bathed often. Sweat and oil glands pour their secretions onto the surface of the skin. The oil, especially, causes extra dirt to cling. Sometimes the oil and dirt clog pores, giving germs a good place to live

Opposite page: A recipe for healthy living should include such items as plenty of sleep in quiet, airy surroundings, clean water, and fresh, unpolluted air.

and multiply, causing pimples to appear. Washing gets rid of the dirt, and it also stimulates the circulation in the blood vessels of the skin. That makes for a healthier, glowing skin. Exercise does the same thing.

Young people are often worried about pimples. If regular washing with soap and water doesn't get rid of pimples, they usually disappear in time. Picking at the pimples is not the answer, for that often makes them worse. Your doctor can sometimes be of help with this problem.

Boys and girls, I want to speak about something else for a moment; something that will be useful in helping you to take good care of yourself. You all know what habits are, don't you? Not sure, Dewey? Well, I'll just say a habit is an action repeated so often that it becomes automatic. Of course you know that there are good habits and bad ones. Naturally, I hope all of your habits are good ones. Now, I know very well that many of the things you have to do are things that are boring or a nuisance. For example, many people are bored by having to brush their teeth.

Yes, Huey, I'll explain how habits fit into all this talk. Habitual actions are automatic, eh? They don't need any thinking on your part, so you can think about other, more interesting things while you perform the habitual action. Let me say just one other thing, boys and girls. The best way to set up any habit is to practice it without exception. If you want to make tooth brushing a habit, brush your teeth every time you are supposed to. Don't say, "I'll do it later." You won't!

What's that, Louie? Oh, very good! Louie wants to know more about caring for his teeth. I was going to take that up with you, so why not now? Your teeth fit together closely in the mouth, with rather small spaces between. This makes for good chewing, but it also causes a problem. Bits of food remain between your teeth, making a good place for decay bacteria to grow. That's why brushing your teeth is so important. Decay bacteria can do a lot of damage in a short time. Of course your teeth look better when they're clean, and if they look better, don't you?

Dewey just asked me how often he should brush his teeth. Dewey, you should see the dentist at least twice a year. He's the one who will tell you how often to brush. Dentists usually suggest brushing after meals, after you have had any sweets, and before you go to bed. The dentist will also show you the right way to brush, and tell you whether to use dental floss in cleaning your teeth. With his good advice and your good care, your teeth can be a great asset for a long, long time.

Boys and girls, talking about teeth made me think about the things we eat. I think this would be a good time for us to talk a bit about our food habits. People are very interested in food. Maybe that's why you hear so many theories about 113

how and what to eat. So many different and often conflicting ideas can make eating seem a very complex problem, but it doesn't have to be. Do you remember when we talked about the Basic Four foods? I'll just remind you that following the Basic Four diet gives you enough of all the nutrients, vitamins, and minerals you need each day. No special foods are needed. Nor should you use vitamin pills unless your doctor tells you to. Another thing please, my friends, and this is very important—if you want to lose weight, you should follow a diet that includes a variety of foods and is low on carbohydrates and fats. Better still, let your doctor check you first and recommend a reducing diet.

Boys and girls, there are so many things I want to discuss with you, and there's so little time! Let me see now, what should come next? Ah, I have it! Aside from food, what enters the body in large amounts? Well, yes, that's true about water. But what else? Right you are Huey, air is the answer!

As you know, far too many places today have polluted air. Cleaning up the air is a job for governments to direct, with the help of industries and individuals like you—and me too, of course. But there are some things about the air we breathe that we should deal with. Rooms in which you work should have the windows open at least a little—yes, even in winter—to allow fresh air to come in. Stale, dry, reheated air can make you sleepy, give you headaches, and pave the way for colds.

People disagree about the temperature in sleeping rooms. A lot of the disagreement results from habit, not from real understanding of the problem. The tem-

These young boys at their school lunch are the picture of good health. How many of them will spoil that picture by taking up smoking?

115

116

Opposite page, left: Statue of Aesculapius, the healer. Ancient Greeks believed he was a god and built temples in his honor. Sick people were brought to the temples for magical healing. Above: The statue is a recreation from his temple at Epidaurus. Opposite page, right: Galen, great Roman physician of the 2nd century. Illustration is the frontispiece from a 16th-century collection of his works.

117

perature of the room should not be as high as it is during the day. It should be cool enough, in fact, to allow some loss of body heat, without chilling the body. Drafts should be avoided. If the room is heated by a gas or liquid fuel heater, a window must be open to prevent the accumulation of carbon monoxide gas, a deadly poison. If the room is air conditioned, make sure you don't have strong air currents—drafts, in other words—sweeping over you.

Talking of ventilation reminds me that I must talk to you about smoking. Boys and girls, I have a package of cigarettes. No, no, I don't smoke! I only brought the package to read to you what's printed on the label. Just listen to this, please. "Warning: The Surgeon General has determined that cigarette smoking is dangerous to your health." Notice, it didn't say "may be dangerous," it said "*is* danger-

Some early medical schools. Above: Corner of a classroom of 500 years ago. Below: A 15th-century engraving of the famous medical school at Salerno, Italy. Opposite page: The anatomy lecture room at the University of Padua, Italy.

Top left: Paracelsus, Swiss physician born in the 15th century, was one of the first to use drugs scientifically for the treatment of disease. Top right: Sculpture of Edward Jenner, 19th-century English physician, vaccinating a child. Jenner's discovery of smallpox vaccination saved countless lives.

ous." No room for doubt in that statement, is there?

Yes, Dewey? You want to know why smoking is dangerous to health? Well, boys and girls, here are a few goodies found by committees of scientists in the United States and England who investigated smoking:

• Cigarette smoking causes lung cancer.

• Cigarette smoking is the most important cause of chronic bronchitis (a lung disease) in the United States.

• Men who smoke cigarettes are much more likely to die of heart attacks than men who do not smoke cigarettes.

• Cigarette smoking is related to other diseases of the heart and blood vessels, as well as to pulmonary emphysema, a disabling disease of the lungs.

Boys and girls, don't you think this is good enough evidence to keep everybody away from cigarette smoking? Of course,

it isn't easy for most people to stop smoking. It's much easier never to start.

Diseases of the heart and blood vessels are a special concern of doctors, because the number of people with these diseases is increasing. The doctors don't all agree on the best way to avoid these problems, but most of them would agree with these rules:

• Eat sensibly. The Basic Four diet can be a help. Avoid overeating to avoid overweight. The heart of the overweight person has to do more work.

• Avoid infections. Mild infections should be treated; teeth should be cleaned and cavities filled.

• Don't smoke.

• Avoid emotional upsets, if possible.

• Avoid overwork. Get enough rest.

• Avoid overexercising.

• See your doctor regularly.

Boys and girls, this may sound funny, but I want to talk with you about the

Top left: Jean Henri Dunant, Swiss philanthropist, helped to found Red Cross after seeing horrors of Battle of Solferino, Italy, in 1859. Top right: Louis Pasteur, French scientist, whose discoveries included vaccination against anthrax and rabies.

right way to see the doctor. You can help him, and yourself, if you have an idea of why he works the way he does.

There is an old joke about a man who had never seen a doctor, until one day when he became very sick. A famous doctor was called. "Where is the pain?" asked the doctor. The sick man opened his eyes, and exclaimed angrily, "If you are really the great doctor everybody says you are, why do you ask me? You should know!"

Doctors do ask a lot of questions for very good reasons. A doctor may have an office full of the most modern equipment, but one of the most valuable of all his tools is the medical history he gets from you. You are an individual, not exactly like any other human being, and the doctor takes that into consideration before he treats you. That's why he must learn all he can about you.

Boys and girls, after our long look at

the body, you realize how many things the doctor must keep in mind about you, especially if he is seeing you for the first time. If a doctor is to learn what is wrong he must know how you feel, how you felt earlier, whether you feel pain, where, and how strongly, what your eating, sleeping, and exercise habits are, and so on. Some of the questions may seem unrelated to your problem, but your answers may help him to pinpoint what is wrong. So, boys and girls, wonder all you like about the doctor's questions, but answer them truthfully and as fully as you can. The doctor is there to help you, but he can only do that with your help.

My friends, you are the lucky owners of remarkable machines—your bodies. The machines have been improving since man first appeared on the earth. You are lucky also to live at a time when great progress is being made in treating disease, and prolonging life. Enjoy it! 121

122   *Fun at the seashore. Good health adds to the enjoyment of our work and our play.*

INDEX